MIND 4 SURVIVAL

HOW TO FACE ANY CRISIS, MINIMIZE UNWANTED STRUGGLE, AND LIVE YOUR BEST POSSIBLE LIFE

BRIAN DUFF

Mind4Survival
How to Face Any Crisis, Minimize Unwanted Struggle, and Live Your Best Possible Life

Copyright © 2025. Brian Duff. All rights reserved.

No part of this publication may be reproduced, distributed, or transmitted in any form or by any means, including photocopying, recording, or other electronic or mechanical methods, without the prior written permission of the copyright holder, except in the case of brief quotations embodied in critical reviews and certain other noncommercial uses permitted by copyright law.

Resilient Publications

ISBN: 979-8-9913093-0-1

Book Design by Transcendent Publishing | TranscendentPublishing.com
Edited by Mary Rembert
Photography by Joe Triplett

This publication is based on the author's personal experience and evolving understanding of the topics discussed. It is meant to be a source of valuable information for the reader. As every situation is unique, the information in this book is meant to supplement, not replace, consultation with a competent professional.

Printed in the United States of America.

DEDICATION

To my father, for always being there when my preps weren't

TABLE OF CONTENTS

Introduction ix
Chapter 1: The Foundation of Preparedness 1
Chapter 2: Maslow's Hierarchy of Needs 21
Chapter 3: Mindset 39
Chapter 4: Bias—The Line Between Perspective and Reality . . . 61
Chapter 5: Situational Awareness and Decision-Making 77
Chapter 6: Survival 101
Chapter 7: Safety: Managing Risk and Opportunity 133
Chapter 8: Self: Eight Truths to Live Your Best Life Possible . . 159
Conclusion 189
How to Get More Help 193
Author's Note 199
Acknowledgments 203
Glossary 205
About the Author 211

BONUS GIFT

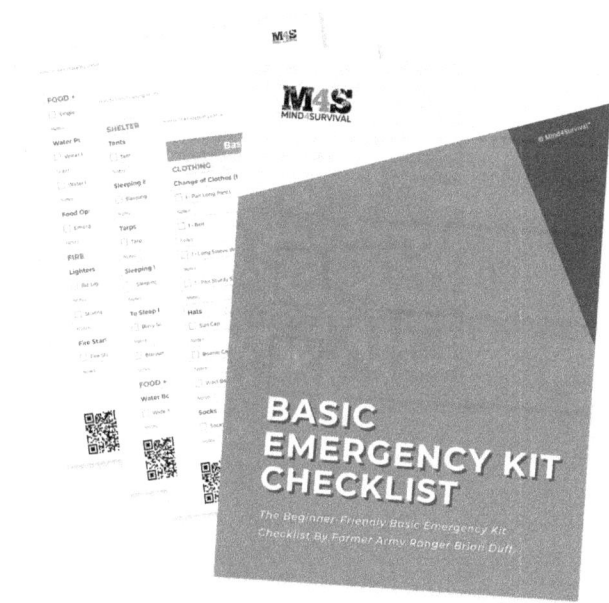

Download your free

Basic Emergency Kit Checklist

Get started keeping your family safe without wasting time and money. Jump-start your preparedness to be ready for whatever happens.

Download the free checklist here:

www.mind4survival.com/startprepping

INTRODUCTION

My parents never hid from me the fact that I was adopted. So, I always wondered whether the way I viewed the world was part of my genetics. When you consider the chaos of the late 1960s in which I was conceived (as the love child of two CIA officers serving in Southeast Asia), the idea of preparedness was likely programmed into my DNA from the start.

For reasons I couldn't explain, I was always on alert, constantly asking myself, "What if?" I was the kid who wore seatbelts when seatbelts weren't required and definitely weren't cool.

Meeting my biological parents clarified a few things for me.

Around age nineteen or twenty, curious as to my origin, I went to the adoption agency in Los Angeles to locate my birth parents. They assigned a counselor to my case and told me it might take a while. About a year later, and after I'd forgotten about it, I received a call. "Hey, we're ready to meet with you," the adoption agency counselor said. "We'll talk with you about your birth parents."

About a month later, I went to the adoption agency to meet with my caseworker. She handed me three pieces of paper:

a very broad description of my birth mother, a very broad description of my birth father, and a list of people and organizations who conducted searches for biological parents. I reached out to a volunteer from the list, who struggled initially to locate them. Finally, a couple of months later, she called, telling me she tracked down the phone number for my biological father.

The first time I spoke with my birth father, the conversation was short, a bit standoffish, and to the point. I was okay with that since I already had a family I loved. But I was still curious about who these people were. I wanted to better understand what made me—me. Thankfully, he was willing to tell me where he thought my birth mother lived, and we left it at that. I took the information back to the investigator, who, after finally identifying my birth mother, gave me her number. After a few deep breaths, I dialed the phone.

"Hi, my name is Brian Duff," I said when she answered. "And I was born February 10th ..."

"... 1968!" she finished. So excited she could hardly speak, she said, "Let me get a pencil and write down your information so I can call you back tomorrow."

Since that call, we've had many conversations, but Mom has yet to tell me exactly what her job was at the CIA. At one point, she gave me a book on Air America (the CIA's air transport program that supported its covert operations in Southeast Asia), and my bio-father later told me she was some sort of security coordinator for the program. So, over time, I have put together bits and pieces.

I eventually discovered more about my bio-father, too. He grew up in West Virginia as a descendant of the McCoy family, from the Hatfield and McCoy feud. He joined the Navy and, in time, went to Vietnam, where he was attached to the Army's Green Berets. After leaving the Navy, he eventually found work with the CIA, where one of his assignments was bugging the Chinese embassy in India. He was also one of the first Americans to hear about the Pueblo Incident when the North Koreans captured a U.S. spy ship in 1968. His final job with the Agency was important enough that the Vietnamese put a bounty on his head. During this time, he rotated between work in Vietnam and leave in Taiwan, where he and my mother connected. His priority was the mission, and neither knew if he would survive.

When my mother discovered she was pregnant, she wanted to give me a chance at life. Knowing that the single-parent option in the 1960s wasn't ideal for all involved, she made the difficult decision to put me up for adoption. As a result, the CIA assigned her to its Los Angeles field office in 1967, and I was born in early 1968.

Thankfully, about a month after I was born, my adoptive parents, a young working-class Los Angeles couple, adopted me, and I was raised as a Northeast L.A. surfer kid. I had a loving father—the nicest, hardest working, and most supportive father I could have hoped for. Mom, on the other hand, was a high-yield nuclear bomb waiting to detonate at a moment's notice. I always knew she loved me and did the best she could with the cards she was dealt, but I didn't realize how much her unpredictable nature impacted my approach to life at a young age. I needed to always be prepared with my mom, and I developed skills and a perspective that would come in handy later.

As a teenager, I saved my first life as a 16-year-old lifeguard—a dream job for a young, safety-minded guy who loves helping people in need. Then, in my early adult years, I worked as a firefighter and paramedic, fighting wildland and structure fires and running thousands of EMS calls. Later, I volunteered and was selected to serve as an Army Ranger with the 75th Ranger Regiment.

Following 9/11, I spent over a decade deployed with the U.S. Government, operating medical clinics across Afghanistan and Uzbekistan, providing high-threat protection for diplomats in Iraq and Pakistan, working with a team of advisors to a rebel army in Africa, and overseeing the guard force at the world's largest embassy in Baghdad, Iraq. After my overseas time, I ground my soul as a corporate executive running a $1B+ international security program and as the director of one of the world's premier tactical and EMS education and training companies.

Eventually, though, the evils of the Washington, DC, beltway bandits and corporate America, along with my post-traumatic stress, became too much to bear. Realizing my only options were to eat a gun or do the difficult work required to heal, I simplified my life, dove into the pain, and began sharing what I learned along the way.

Looking back now, I realize I have spent most of my adult life traveling the country and the world, unknowingly trying to protect myself by protecting others. It's during those travels and my series of close calls and lucky mistakes that I was able to learn from some of the best, survive some of the worst, and, in so doing, develop my mind for survival philosophy that I'm sharing with you.

Preparedness–Past and Present

Whatever your background, if you're living in America or another developed nation, you probably have it really good compared to the rest of the world.

We have it so good that it's easy to take the need to prepare for granted. Case in point: consider the freak-out over toilet paper a few years ago.

People saw the holes on the shelves and realized that our just-in-time supply chain system had started to wobble. Until then, it had kept us all fed, fat, and relatively happy, which has always worked well. As it wobbled, people went bananas and fought over toilet paper! Can you imagine the craziness that would have happened had the supply chain truly *collapsed*?

Now, between the wars, pandemics, struggling economies, supply-chain issues, food shortages, and political turmoil, it's easy to feel anxious, worried, and insecure. The days and years following 9/11 are providing a wake-up call that reveals one chilling truth: most people are *not* as prepared as they should be.

Of course, the need for preparedness is nothing new. Up until modern times and first-world conveniences, preparing for tomorrow was a regular part of daily life. People didn't have supermarkets, fast-responding emergency services, or (by today's standard) what we would consider qualified medical care. By and large, people had to be self-reliant because no one was coming to help them in good times or bad.

The same holds true for much of our world today. Unlike the developed world, people in struggling nations often live in a permanent state of collapse. They *have to* prepare because, in their world, even on the best of days, there are holes on the shelves.

During my travels around the globe, I witnessed firsthand the daily struggle for survival. I have seen:

- disabled people literally crawling on their hands and knees through the mud to get food
- women with no other options than filling their water jugs at the same place where a crocodile ate their friend the day before
- children trying unsuccessfully to earn money for food by digging up landmines for terrorists

Now, while many of us in the U.S. and much of the first world don't face these same kinds of issues and haven't had to think about preparedness in nearly a century, current times mandate that we *all* be more self-reliant and prepared for whatever may come.

Not Just for Preppers

On the far end of the preparedness spectrum are the preppers, like you might see on reality TV. To be fully transparent, I lean this way. I genuinely enjoy searching for and having supplies. I like having long-term food storage, extra clothes, water filters, home security systems and plans, self-defense gear, and alternative energy options. My tools are all the same brand and use the same battery. This kind of uniformity makes sense to preppers like me (and yes, I have backup batteries and backups to my backup batteries). As preppers like to say, "Two is one, one is none."

"Preppers" live by a certain philosophy. Similar to those who homestead, they want to be independent. I define a prepper as a person who believes in preparing for emergencies or disasters by gaining the knowledge, skills, and resources and making plans to ensure survival, minimize unwanted struggle, and live their best possible life. At its core, the prepper lifestyle is one of self-sufficiency and finding ways to be more resilient. Preppers want their first fallback and disaster assistance to be themselves.

Now, while every prepper is into preparedness, not every preparedness-minded person is a prepper. Preppers like me attend weekend retreats with classes, watch survival videos, and seek out information on stuff like medicinal plants and water purification. We install longer screws into hinges, reinforce door jambs, and add security systems and shatterproof window tinting to help secure our homes. And for most of us, if our house and accompanying food forest aren't built on top of a three-thousand-square-foot bunker, trust me, we are working toward that goal. There is a lot to glean from tribes like ours, but that doesn't mean you have to join our tribe.

You might simply be a person who wants to be more prepared. You don't want to spend your whole life thinking about the worst-case scenario, nor do you want to be considered a prepper. You just want to attain what you feel is a reasonable level of preparedness so you can feel more confident about your future.

If that sounds like you, you're in the right place. This book is for the full spectrum of preparedness-minded people—from those who may not know where to begin with their preparedness to preppers who want to fine-tune their approach. I won't tell you to buy a bunker, an arsenal, or a mountain of freeze-dried food. What I am going to do, though, is provide you with my perspective and mindset on preparedness—a perspective gained through decades of struggle and survival.

Empowering You to Live Your Best Possible Life

Our modern times have highlighted an absolute fact—which also happens to be the first noble truth in Buddhism—that "life is suffering."[1] Suffering is defined by Webster's as "to be forced to endure."[2] So, suffering equates to and can be further defined as unwanted struggle.

Being born is a struggle. Getting up when you're knocked down is a struggle. Getting going when the going isn't easy is a struggle. Watching your loved ones struggle can be a struggle. Struggle, it turns out, is *not* just a developing nation thing. It's an every-nation and every-person thing.

Everyone goes through crap. At some point, we all feel anxiety and uncertainty, not 100 percent confident in what the future holds for ourselves or our crazy world. It's totally normal to have these feelings, and I'd be concerned if you didn't have them.

---

[1] Donald S. Lopez, "Four Noble Truths," Encyclopædia Britannica, June 27, 2024, https://www.britannica.com/topic/Four-Noble-Truths.
[2] "Suffers Definition & Meaning," Merriam-Webster, accessed August 11, 2024, https://www.merriam-webster.com/dictionary/suffers.

That said, I did not write this book to make you fearful and anxious—just the opposite. I wrote it to empower you with the confidence to live *your best possible life* by being prepared and not scared. I wrote *Mind4Survival* because I've seen too many good people struggle simply because they didn't know how to prepare themselves and their families for difficult times.

My Mind4Survival philosophy stems from my desire to ensure everybody understands the mindset of preparedness, and that's what this book does. It teaches you how to develop an effective mindset to keep you and your family safe while making the most of every opportunity. That's important because being prepared is a liberating, stress-reducing mindset to enjoy when viewed through the correct lens.

This book is so foundational and unique in the world of preparedness that you can use it with any preparedness system. It's the cement that will hold all of your preparedness, thoughts, and efforts together. *Mind4Survival* sets the stage for looking at life, evaluating its situations, and preparing to make the best of whatever comes your way.

In the first few chapters of this book, we'll look at what preparedness actually entails, how it relates to your human needs, and my Mind4Survival philosophy, which boils down to five key areas: Mindset, Situational Awareness, Survival, Safety, and Self. We'll then dive deep into each of these and how they play out. I'll offer you practical tools along the way.

Ultimately, I hope you gain a new, empowering, and confidence-boosting mindset and the knowledge you need to face any crisis, minimize unwanted struggles, and live your best possible life.

While this book is overflowing with information to help you lead a more positive and prepared life, it is not the end of the journey. Instead, while it's an excellent start, it is just the beginning. Once you understand how to sharpen and refine your mindset, it's time to put that mindset to work, learning the more granular, hands-on side of preparedness that is specific to your situation.

That, however, is putting the cart before the horse. Rest assured, when you get to the end of this book, I'll have opportunities for you to expand your Mind4Survival even more. In the meantime, you're ready for your first overwhelm-reducing preparedness rule: There is no need to try to prepare for *everything*. By preparing for *something*, you are inadvertently preparing for everything—and that's empowering.

By picking up this book, you are preparing for something. Therefore, you are preparing for everything. Congratulations! You've got this!

CHAPTER 1

THE FOUNDATION OF PREPAREDNESS

When I was a young child, I remember my mother telling me that my grandfather was a violent and abusive alcoholic who would go ballistic at the drop of a hat. Now, I don't ever recall seeing that in him, but he also went through shock treatments in the 1960s, so maybe they worked.

Mom told me that when she was a child, her father would yell and go nuts while driving. As a result, she thought her mother might jump out of the car at any moment. She said that whenever they drove anywhere, she always had her coloring book and doll in her arms—in case her mother decided to dive out of the car. My mother was prepared to follow her and was always ready to jump out if the chance arose. She finished her statement to me with something like, "You always have to be ready."

At the time, I recall thinking how crazy that sounded, and yet how it also made sense and felt comforting to consider. I don't know if that was my "Aha!" moment, but I remember her telling me to "always be ready" really registered with me, a guy whose life was wiring him that way. What I didn't know was what it actually meant to "be ready" and what I was supposed to be ready for.

What Is Preparedness?

As you work through the chapters in this book, it's important that we speak the same language. So, before you go any further, I want to ensure we have a commonality of terminology, particularly on the definition of preparedness.

Department of Homeland Security Definition of Preparedness

The challenge with defining preparedness is that it has no standard definition. For example, the Department of Homeland Security (DHS), which you think would have nailed it, defines preparedness as "a continuous cycle of planning, organizing, training, equipping, exercising, evaluating, and taking corrective action in an effort to ensure effective coordination during incident response."[3] Besides being a long-winded definition, what are they getting at there? What are they really telling us? If we boil it down to its essence, DHS is telling us that its goal is to ensure effective coordination during incident response... *Hmm ... okay ...?*

Yes, they are supposed to coordinate assets and resources, but I don't see anything there that indicates saving lives or reducing people's struggles. Maybe that's the implied end goal, and as Hurricane Katrina, Helene, and other disasters illustrate, it's

---

[3] "Plan and Prepare for Disasters: Homeland Security," U.S. Department of Homeland Security, August 1, 2024, https://www.dhs.gov/archive/plan-and-prepare-disasters.

not showing up in their definition. I am totally on board with the "continuous cycle of planning, organizing, training, equipping, exercising, evaluating, and taking corrective action" part, but they kind of lose me at the end because they don't have a well-defined purpose and end goal. Why do all that planning, organizing, and "effective coordinating" without stating something other than an administrative goal?

New York State Department of Health Definition of Preparedness

The New York State Department of Health defines preparedness as "the steps you take to make sure you are safe before, during, and after an emergency or a natural disaster."[4] That definition works if you are preparing for an emergency or a natural disaster, but real preparedness isn't just being ready for something negative to happen.

The Mind4Survival Definition of Preparedness

My definition takes on a more comprehensive twist: preparedness is all the efforts taken to ensure survival, minimize unwanted struggle, and live your best possible life.

To live your best life, you want to prepare for opportunities, too, so you are at your best to capitalize on that opportunity when it occurs. Maybe you are saving money and stockpiling three months' worth of food in anticipation of starting a business or pursuing a new certification to open up better opportunities at your place of employment. Neither is an emergency nor a

---

[4] "Department of Health," What is emergency preparedness?, March 2008, https://www.health.ny.gov/environmental/emergency/people_with_disabilities/preparedness.htm.

natural disaster, but both should be prepared for if you have set those as goals.

Preparedness also involves *looking* for opportunities to improve your situation or improve your life overall by minimizing the negative. Again, this type of preparedness doesn't involve catastrophic events; it is just ways to improve your situation—modifying your home so that you can age in safety and comfort or perhaps creating a plan for getting out of debt.

The Goals of Preparedness

Now that you understand that preparedness is a comprehensive approach to living that empowers you to face any challenge with confidence and resilience, it's time to focus on the goals of preparedness.

At the core of my preparedness philosophy are three pivotal goals that outline what we're trying to accomplish. Those goals, which will seem very familiar because they're based on the definition of preparedness, are survival, minimizing unwanted struggle, and living your best possible life. Each of these goals builds upon the previous, creating a foundation for a life where you not only survive but thrive.

The First Goal of Preparedness: Survival

Survival is the first goal of preparedness because, without survival, there is nothing left. If you don't survive, you're not around to prepare or do anything else, such as live your best life.

There are two basic aspects to survival: avoiding massive trauma and maintaining homeostasis. Massive trauma instantaneously ends survival and includes events that are so powerful there is no future concern for the person impacted—because they are dead. We must avoid that to get to the next aspect of survival, which is homeostasis.

If you don't instantly die from massive trauma, your next survival hurdle will be maintaining homeostasis. In other words, your body is always working to maintain an equilibrium. If it is low on blood, it speeds up your heart to make sure oxygen gets to your brain. When you get too hot, you sweat. When you get too cold, you shiver. If you don't drink enough, your throat gets dry. When you don't eat, you get hungry. The fact is, your body is constantly adjusting to keep everything in balance so you function as optimally as possible.

Unfortunately, the human body cannot always compensate for the problems it experiences. If bleeding isn't stopped, for example, a person can suffer brain damage and death. Likewise, exposure to extremely cold weather eventually leads to hypothermia, which leads to difficulty functioning, which leads to—yep, you guessed it—death.

Sweating can only go so far in keeping a person cool, and without intervention, overheating can lead to permanent injury or even death. The same goes for the lack of water and food. Go long enough without either, and our bodies will no longer be able to compensate and adjust, resulting in death.

Therefore, survival is a two-step process: avoid massive trauma and maintain homeostasis. Once survival is taken care of, the next goal of preparedness is to minimize the unwanted struggle in your life.

The Second Goal of Preparedness: Minimize Unwanted Struggle

We've already covered that the First Noble Truth of Buddhism teaches that "life is suffering."[5] Suffering and unwanted struggle happen when you are forced to endure something.

I don't want to be forced to do anything, let alone endure something, and I definitely don't want to endure unwanted struggle. I want to *choose* to endure something.

If struggle is involved, I want to choose how and why I do it. Unwanted struggle is something you are *forced* to endure, but wanted struggle is something you *choose* to endure. And yes, wanted struggle can include suffering, in which case you are "forcing yourself" to endure the struggle.

Unwanted struggle includes and is definitely not limited to health problems, financial difficulties, disasters, personal loss, relationship issues, heartache, addiction, and anything that prevents you from surviving, struggling less, and living your best life possible.

Wanted struggle can include working your way through college, being a single mother with two jobs, being a mechanic father turning wrenches in the driveway, eating healthy, exercising, or training with your preparedness gear.

You intentionally choose wanted struggle, hoping to improve your life by doing it. Wanted struggle can help you grow and

---

[5] Barbara O'Brien, "Do You Know the First Noble Truth of Buddhism?," Learn Religions, August 13, 2018, https://www.learnreligions.com/the-first-noble-truth-450089.

be rewarded for your effort. In my case, I'm a hermit, and coming out of my cave can definitely be a struggle. However, to live a more fulfilling life, I need to do just that. When I force myself to get out and do things, I usually have a great time and am happy I did. Knowing this is typically the end result, however, still doesn't make it any easier the next time I force myself to go out—it remains a wanted struggle.

Working on my own preparedness can also be a wanted struggle. I want to do it, and I struggle to get it done. Once it's done, though, I'm happy and more confident because I am better prepared. When we accomplish our goals through wanted struggle, we are rewarded by a dopamine release of success.

While typically unwelcome, you can also experience growth from unwanted struggle. This includes things like health issues, the loss of your home, financial difficulties, family problems, a car wreck, violent crime, and so on. While we are intentional about wanted struggle, unwanted struggle is something we prefer to avoid. That's why you must prepare—to minimize and eliminate it.

The Third Goal of Preparedness: Live Your Best Possible Life

When you successfully achieve the first two goals of preparedness—survival and minimizing unwanted struggle—you will likely find yourself in a better position to achieve the third goal of preparedness: leading a longer, happier, and healthier life.

The opportunity to achieve the third goal is the reward for successfully achieving the first two goals of preparedness.

Striving to live your best possible life is where you can climb the pyramid of life and experience love, belonging, and fulfillment of your true potential—and, in my opinion, *that is what life is all about!*

The Success Formula

Now that we understand the goals of preparedness, the question is, how do we succeed at achieving those goals? The opportunity to be successful at anything is, as shown in my success formula, based on capability and luck, with capability being the ability to do something.

When it comes to successful preparedness, surviving, minimizing unwanted struggle, and living your best possible life relies on your capability (mindset + ability) combined with any good or bad luck that heads your way. Therefore, success can be calculated as:

$$\textbf{Capability + Luck}^{+/-} = \textbf{Chance of Success}$$

The success formula shows that by improving what you can control—namely, your mindset and ability—you are better positioned to overcome bad luck when it shows up. Likewise, by improving your mindset and ability, you can capitalize on good luck when it comes your way.

Remember, preparedness is not just focused on the bad. It is also about maximizing the good in your life as well. Ultimately, it's your ability to make the most of either bad or good luck, which lies within your capability.

Some will argue that we create our own luck through preparedness. I will counter that by saying that we don't create luck. We create increased opportunities for mindset and the ability to capitalize on the very nuanced and sometimes unconsciously recognized opportunities that present themselves.

For example, consider someone who, without appearing to think, reacts nearly instantaneously to avoid a threat—like a person who dives out of the way of an oncoming bus or automobile. Some might say that person is lucky, while others conclude their mindset and ability helped them sidestep a moment of bad luck. The fact is our individual perspectives prevent us from seeing the true or objective reality, which refers to anything that exists independent of our perspective-filled, conscious thought.[6]

The Factors of Success

You can achieve your preparedness goals by maximizing the three factors of success: mindset, ability, and luck. This is where you pit your controllable factors of success—mindset and ability—against the factor of luck, both good and bad, which is uncontrollable and, as such, should never be counted on as part of your preparedness.

You minimize the negative effects of luck while maximizing the positive by maximizing the first two factors of success: mindset and ability. By maximizing mindset and ability, you eliminate any concern or need for luck. Therefore, when you prepare to overcome adversity, you are preparing by doing your best to make the most of your mindset and ability.

---

[6] "Objectivity," Internet encyclopedia of philosophy, accessed August 11, 2024, https://iep.utm.edu/objectiv/.

THE FACTORS OF SUCCESS

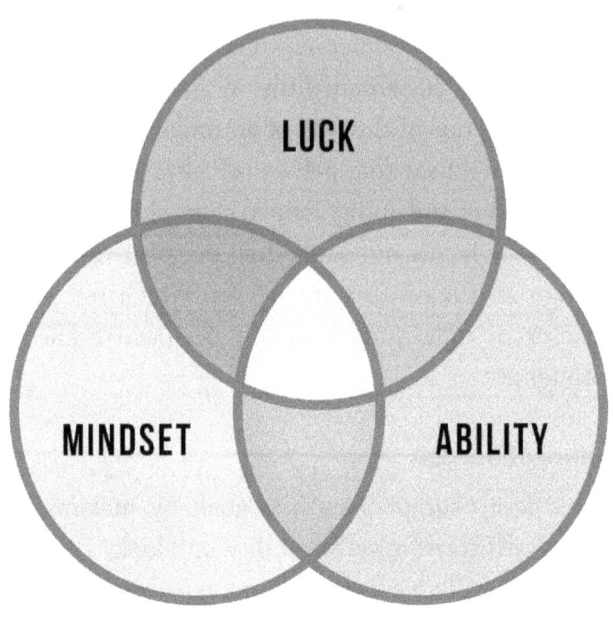

The First Factor of Success: Mindset

I define mindset as your mental readiness and awareness, which shapes how you make sense of and interpret yourself, the world around you, and your situation within that world. Are you upbeat and happy, or do you view things through a veil of despair? Mindset also influences how people think and act in response to a situation, and for those who want to prepare, it sets us on our path to becoming better prepared.

Some people start on the preparedness path because it is in their fundamental wiring to do so. Others have a personal epiphany or "Aha!" moment later in life. The "Aha!" moment is when you realize and accept that you may not be as prepared as you wish you were. And it's your mindset that determines your acceptance and response to your epiphany moment.

One significant piece of my Mind4Survival philosophy is directly connected to mindset. It's called perspective.

Perspective is a belief or opinion about the reality of something or a situation. When it comes to preparedness, perspective is a person's feeling about how prepared they are. While feelings can be based on fact, they are not reliant upon them. This leads many people to believe they are prepared when they are, unfortunately, woefully unprepared.

In the end, it's crucial to remember that your perspective—individually and in groups—does not always equal reality. Your perspective is unique and is skewed by how you perceive someone, something, or a situation. Likewise, your filter of perception is made up of your experiences, biases, culture, upbringing, etc. Everything you perceive factors into who you are—your personality, the fabric in the fiber of your being—and has the potential to skew your understanding of reality (perspective). Your perception can make you believe you are always right, others are always wrong, and your preparedness is 100 percent ready to go—even when none of that is true.

Think about it this way: if you and I were standing out in a field, looking at the trees surrounding it, we would not see the same thing because I have color vision problems. In fact, with everyone's different angles of view, strengths of vision, fields of vision, lazy eyes, astigmatisms, color vision, etc., the odds are, like fingerprints, none of us see the world exactly the same. Therefore, if we were all standing in a field looking at trees together, none of us would see the trees in the same way.

The fact is, everybody walking around the world today has a different perspective of reality. Everybody perceives the world differently—literally. Due to the individuality of human nature, we all perceive the world—and the reality within it—differently than one another, even if that difference is only the thinnest one degree of difference of shade and separation.

On top of physically seeing reality differently from one person to another, everyone heaps on all the other stuff—biases, culture, background, and so on—which further differentiates our individual perceptions. This skewed perception makes our views of reality flawed because we are not seeing the *true* reality. We're experiencing it through a filter of bias and seeing our individual versions, our perspectives of reality.

Your mindset determines what you do in response to your "Aha!" moment. Do you take your newfound realization seriously? Do you say, "Hey, I believe I can be better prepared, so let me see how I can improve my readiness?"

Sometimes, an epiphany makes people feel safer, more confident, more self-reliant, and better prepared to care for themselves and their loved ones. Most likely, you're here because you want the confidence that being better prepared brings. (If that's you, awesome! Congratulations on your newfound mindset and working toward freedom from anxiety, worry, and fear.)

Other times, however, the "Aha!" moment causes people to feel overwhelmed, anxious, and totally unprepared to take care of themselves and their loved ones when it matters most. (And if that's you, that's fine, too, because it's totally normal to feel worried even after an "Aha!" preparedness moment. Most people do.)

If your "I've got to get prepared" moment makes you feel a bit stressed out, remember that you don't have to prepare for everything. You just have to take a step forward. Reading this book is one important step. By doing so, you are leveling up, becoming more knowledgeable, and, as a result, being better prepared.

As you go through this process, remember that mindset is controllable—meaning you can improve your mindset should you decide to do so. You have a choice to either be complacent and accept unwanted struggle as it happens or to be proactive in addressing unwanted struggle by asking yourself the hard questions that truly matter to your preparedness:

- Are you willing to look and think outside of your comfort zone in an effort to become better prepared?
- Are you willing to consider that you may not be as capable as you believe and, therefore, not as prepared as you think?
- Are you also willing to consider that you may only be partially right on topics that you're certain about and have room for 100 percent improvement on others?

If you are willing to be personally honest and look at yourself critically, you will be in a much better position to avoid pitfalls such as overconfidence and bias that can lead to a catastrophe during times of struggle. Ultimately, as Horace, the Roman poet, said: "Rule your mind, or it will rule you."[7]

The Second Factor of Success: Ability

The second factor of success is ability, which I define as having the knowledge, skill, and resources to do something.

Knowledge × Skill × Resources = Ability

Knowledge and skill are the internal components of ability, and your combination of these determines how well you can do something. While knowledge and skill are internal components, they rely on resources, which are the external components you use to succeed in the goals of preparedness. They include:

- books you use to expand your mind
- the air you breathe, which keeps your brain alive
- tools, materials, and finances you use to keep a roof over your head
- water to keep your body hydrated
- food required for sustenance

Fortunately, as with mindset, you can control your ability. Yes, we may have limitations, but over time, we can improve and hone our abilities through increased knowledge and skill. In

---

[7] "A Quote by Horatius," Goodreads, accessed August 11, 2024, https://www.goodreads.com/quotes/980768-rule-your-mind-or-it-will-rule-you.

other words, we can all improve our capability to survive, suffer less, and live more confident, worry-free lives.

The Third Factor of Success: Luck

Finally, we have the third factor of success: luck. The Roman statesman Cicero is credited with the quote, "Fortune is not only blind herself, but blinds the people she has embraced."[8] In other words, luck is uncertain and can turn against you. There is no rhyme or reason to it.

There are no guarantees when it comes to luck. With luck, you have only uncontrollable, random chance. In fact, even if you cross your fingers, the only sure thing when it comes to luck is that, unlike mindset and ability, it is totally uncontrollable. Since luck is 100 percent uncontrollable, it is an unreliable factor of success.

Now, I personally love good luck—who doesn't? When it helps, luck is awesome. When it causes problems, especially when it turns a situation from bad to worse, luck totally sucks. Therefore, because luck is unpredictable and uncontrollable, you must not depend upon it as a factor of success, especially when it comes to preparedness.

To achieve your preparedness goals as effectively as possible, you must work to maximize the factors of preparedness that you can control and, as a result, improve upon. Because no matter how much you increase your ability and improve your mindset, you always need to be ready to overcome luck.

---

[8] "Marcus Tullius Cicero Quote," AZ Quotes, accessed August 11, 2024, https://www.azquotes.com/quote/1137342.

The Success Formula in Action

The success formula, Capability + Luck$^{+/-}$ = Chance of Success, can be applied in both real and hypothetical scenarios to illustrate how improving the controllable factors of success (mindset and ability) can mitigate the effects of luck and enhance your overall chance of success. Here are examples of both types:

Success Example 1: Emergency Evacuation During a Natural Disaster

Scenario: John, a software engineer in his 40s, lives with his family in an area prone to wildfires. Over the years, he has taken steps to improve his preparedness by educating himself on fire safety, creating an evacuation plan, and regularly practicing it with his family. He has also assembled emergency kits for his home and car.

Capability: John's mindset is proactive. He believes in being prepared. He demonstrates his ability through his knowledge of wildfire safety, his skill in creating and executing an evacuation plan, and the resources he has assembled in his emergency kits.

Luck: Unfortunately, in the middle of a hot and windy night, a wildfire unexpectedly breaks out near John's neighborhood, forcing an immediate evacuation. To the dismay of those fleeing the rapidly approaching flames, the fire has engulfed the primary evacuation route (bad luck) out of the area.

Outcome: Fortunately for John's family, John prepared ahead of time (wanted struggle) and identified an alternate route out of the area. Therefore, John's knowledge of the area and his skill at planning have increased his capability, allowing him and his family to evacuate quickly and safely, minimizing the impact of bad luck on them. While his preparations didn't prevent the wildfire (unwanted struggle), they did significantly improve his chance of success in overcoming his bad luck and the adverse, life-threatening conditions he was faced with.

Success Example 2: Job Opportunity

Scenario: Alice, a financially struggling single mother, is employed in a competitive field where advancements are rare. Recently, she became excited to learn that a promotion opportunity is opening in her company. Knowing the competition will be tough, she spends weeks studying after the kids go to bed (wanted struggle), improving her skills related to the new position, and networking within her industry (more wanted struggle).

Capability: Alice's mindset is one of growth and ambition. Her ability is enhanced by her dedication to increasing her knowledge and learning new skills relevant to the promotion, as well as cultivating professional relationships that could sway the decision in her favor.

Luck: When the time comes to apply for the promotion, it turns out that one of the key decision-makers is someone Alice impressed during her networking efforts (good luck).

Outcome: Alice's improved capabilities put her in an excellent position to be considered for the promotion. The unexpected connection with the decision-maker complements her qualifications, tipping the scales in her favor. While her effort to improve her knowledge and skills made her a strong candidate, regardless, it was her networking good luck that allowed her to capitalize on the opportunity and significantly increase her chances of success.

These examples demonstrate how enhancing one's capability through improving mindset and ability can significantly affect outcomes, even when the uncontrollable factor of luck plays a role. The Mind4Survival success formula underscores the importance of focusing on what we can control while acknowledging that luck, something we shouldn't count on, will always be a variable, sometimes working in our favor and other times against us.

The Fundamentals of Preparedness

Preparedness establishes the foundation for you to capitalize on opportunity. So, if preparedness sets the stage for helping you to lead a better life, what constitutes preparedness? What makes up its true foundation?

The foundation of preparedness is made up of your capability, which is based on the controllable factors of the success formula: mindset and ability. You also control how solid your foundation of preparedness is. The more work (wanted struggle) you put in to enhance your mindset and ability, the greater, more solid, and better established your foundation of preparedness that you build for yourself will be. And by building a solid foundation of preparedness, you can better mitigate and recover from any harm that may threaten you.

Throughout this book, you will continue to explore how to be successful by being prepared. Along the way, you will be guided by the Mind4Survival (M4S) fundamentals of preparedness:

- Mindset
- Situational Awareness
- Survival

- Safety
- Self

As you can see, mindset is at the center and influences every other part of preparedness, but all the parts are essential. In fact, all five fundamentals connect seamlessly to our needs as humans.

THE FUNDAMENTAL OF PREPAREDNESS

CHAPTER 2

MASLOW'S HIERARCHY OF NEEDS

The African monsoon dumped a deluge of water that quickly overpowered my Toyota Land Cruiser's windshield wipers' ability to keep the soaked outside world at bay. Visibility was only a few yards at best, and even that was difficult. As the Land Cruiser slogged through a muddy, flooded street, something in my limited vision didn't seem quite right. I couldn't see what it was until I was right upon it. In shock, I slammed on my brakes just in the nick of time.

The "it" was a tiny, middle-aged woman on her hands and knees, crawling across the road. She was unable to walk or even sit upright. Her only option in life was to crawl everywhere she went. She wore two pairs of shitty gas station flip-flops, the kind that have toe pieces that rip through the foam, leaving you with a flip-flop blowout. Yes. She wore one pair on her hands, and the other was duct-taped to her knees.

She also wore an old rope tied around her waist. The rope trailed behind her, anchored to a mud-caked burlap sack full of groceries. This woman crawled through life on her hands and knees, duct-taped to shitty flip-flops because that was the best she had. She was determined to care for her needs, regardless of her physical limitations. Her only option for survival was to face her struggle by crawling through life, one miserable muddy inch at a time.

Seeing this woman was, for me, a stark reminder that many people in the world are simply fighting to claim their basic human needs. Now, even on my worst days, when I struggle to find the motivation to do something to further my life, I often think back to the little lady crawling on her hands and knees through the streets of mud. If she can do all she did, certainly I can do whatever task I'm putting off.

Still, motivation is a funny thing. Somewhere along the way, as we grow more comfortable, we can also become more complacent. This is explained, in part, by Maslow's Hierarchy of Needs.

Needs and Preparedness

Abraham Maslow was an American psychologist best known for his 1943 article "A Theory of Human Motivation," which outlines what we now know as Maslow's Hierarchy of Needs.[9] Maslow's theory is most often portrayed as a five-level pyramid,

---

[9] Alexis Ubilla, "A Theory of Human Motivation - Abraham H Maslow - Psychological Review Vol 50 No 4 July 1943," Academia.edu, November 20, 2014, https://www.academia.edu/9415670/A_Theory_of_Human_Motivation_Abraham_H_Maslow_Psychological_Review_Vol_50_No_4_July_1943.

with levels ranging from foundational, physiological survival needs to self-actualization, which is the highest representation of needs. According to Maslow, these are the instinctual requirements that motivate our human behavior.

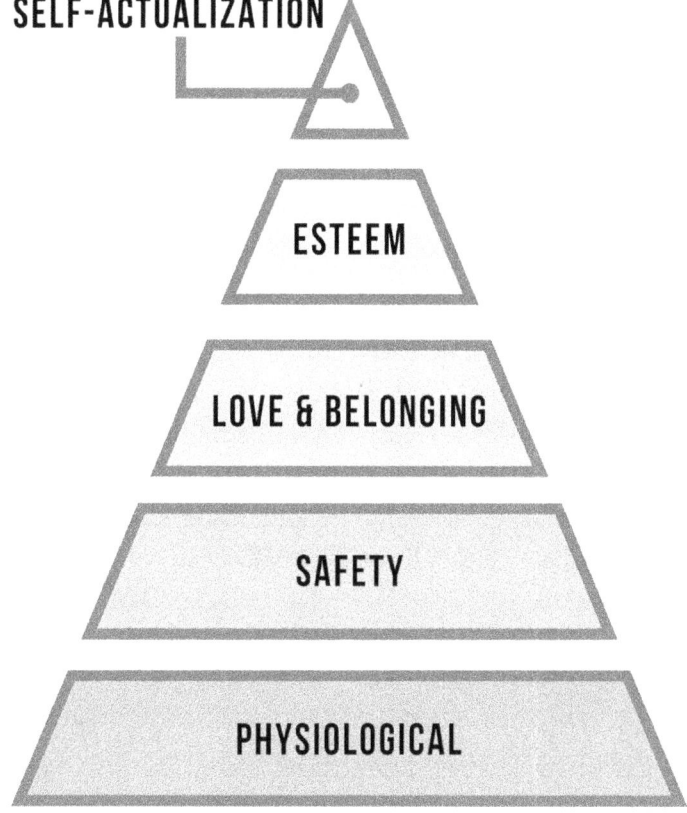

Maslow separates our needs into two categories: deficiency and growth needs. Deficiency needs are represented in the bottom two levels of Maslow's pyramid, and they are deprivation-based: not having enough food or water to survive, for example. Our deficiency needs are all based upon our ability to maintain equilibrium and physiological homeostasis: you need your body to pump blood, you need a certain amount of water and oxygen, etc. In time, we must also meet our safety needs, so we observe laws, buy or rent homes, and work for money to sustain our lives.

In a nutshell, our deficiency needs must be met to survive, and the longer those needs go unmet, the greater our motivation to fulfill them. Conversely, as our needs are met, our instinctual motivation to meet them diminishes, and we can turn our focus to other unmet needs. In short, as we reach and maintain homeostasis in one area, our motivation and focus shift to meet other needs.

Growth needs are represented in the upper three levels, and these are needs that come as a natural yearning to grow as human beings. These needs are more emotional than physiological. Referring back to Maslow's Pyramid, these needs range from our relationships to our achievements and—if we're fortunate enough—self-actualization and personal fulfillment.

Breaking Down the Pyramid

The base of Maslow's pyramid represents your most basic physiological survival needs. From there, his hierarchy progresses up through the pyramid and on to other needs:

- Physiological needs: these are your homeostatic needs, such as the need for oxygen, shelter, water, sleep, nourishment, etc.
- Safety: with your short-term physiological needs handled, you now need long-term solutions to maintain safety, security, and stability for yourself, your family, finances, health, home, etc.
- Love and belonging: once you're safe and secure, you can effectively focus on your interpersonal relationships with friends, family, and so on.
- Esteem: this addresses the need to have distinct self-esteem, achieve great things, and have the respect of others.
- Self-actualization: for those of us fortunate enough to evolve beyond ourselves, self-actualization involves fulfilling your true potential through the culmination of your lived experience, mindset, and relationship with the human condition.

How do these needs relate to preparedness? Unfortunately, our efforts to rise up to the top of our individual pyramids can be totally derailed and swallowed up by circumstances. Our forward momentum and the things we do in life are often stifled by lower-level problems that pull us and our focus back down the pyramid. Think of what the woman in my story had to do to simply survive. In many ways, she was stuck in the deficiency needs due to her situation.

No matter how much we are able to progress to higher growth needs, our setbacks, failures, and circumstances often create a yo-yo effect in terms of "traveling the pyramid." We don't meet a need and move on, never to revisit that need again. Our needs ebb and flow as we encounter the circumstances of life. Relationships, careers, fortunes, and health all rise and fall, as do our needs, which is why I believe we are best served by following a holistic, 360-degree approach to our preparedness and life overall.

Later in his career, Maslow realized a flaw with his hierarchy—it was too linear and rigid. Job losses, family drama, natural disasters—there are so many ways your circumstances can thwart your ability to climb the pyramid. For example, if you're struggling to provide food for your family, you're likely not concerned with earning a debatably useful graduate degree or finding a cure for cancer. Your focus will understandably and most likely be on feeding your family to ensure their base physiological needs are met.

That said, there are those who place their esteem and self-actualization (growth needs) over some of their more basic physiological needs. For example, we all know people who risk their family for a career. Then there are those, like the Irish hunger-strikers of the early 1980s, who risked their lives for a cause. For better or worse, these people placed more importance on their higher-level pursuits than their lower-level and base physiological needs.

While slightly flawed, Maslow's original pyramid still provides immense value because the biological requirements for human survival must largely be provided and maintained before other needs. Similarly, when it comes to preparedness or lack of it, the desire to avoid thinking about and facing crisis can almost surely result in unnecessary struggle and difficulty ascending the pyramid.

As a result, our emotional desire, when allowed to override our preparedness, can ultimately impede our ability to provide what we need to enjoy a longer, more fulfilling life. I am not suggesting that we should all run scared or live in fear—just the opposite. This is about empowerment, remember?

With a nod back to our example of someone on a hunger strike, your emotions can override how you approach human nature, but only for a period of time. Denying yourself food and water, in this instance, will eventually catch up with you. You are either hunger-striking until someone intervenes, or you're committing suicide. Your physiological needs shape how you view and interact with the world and, therefore, must be met to ensure your survival.

One area that Maslow and I disagree on, however, is the issue of sex as a basic survival need. Maslow considered this a physiological need, and while I believe that you may feel like you have to have sex, it's not essential for survival. I don't see a bunch of celibate people dropping dead in the streets from not having sex. In my opinion, sex should, depending on a person's perspective, be a love/belonging or esteem-based need and maybe have to do with self-actualization. Regardless, outside of the survival of the species, sex at the individual level is not essential. When it comes to physiological needs, they should only consist of needs that are required for the survival of the *individual*.

So why even explain Maslow's theory and hierarchy if I am poking holes in some of it? Because foundationally, Maslow is largely accurate and on point, and because his hierarchy helps us further understand the goals and five fundamentals of preparedness outlined in Chapter 1.

Physiological Needs

Do you remember the first goal of preparedness that you must achieve? You have to survive any event that would otherwise kill you. That is why mindset is so important. If you don't have the right mindset on how you approach certain aspects of your day, you may not survive the drive home from work (there are any number of statistics on distracted driving fatalities).

Your mindset needs to detect as much informational input as possible because that sets the tone for how you approach the world. In terms of preparedness, if you're not in the right mindset, you may not see the approaching threat, and if you do see it, you may not recognize it as a threat, neither of which is good for you or those who depend on you.

Mindset encompasses how you approach, absorb, and interact with the world. It's your mindset that, when in the right alignment with your situation, can help you maximize the positive. It can also help you overcome your biases and serve as your best line of defense to do so. Without a good mindset, you are more likely to allow yourself to get sucked in by the negative aspects of the human condition and, as a result, not see or understand true reality for what it is.

By default, our reality baseline is already skewed, so it's a question of just how skewed it is and how skewed we perceive it to be. The only tool we have to defend against anything like that is our mindset. Mindset is the most important aspect of preparedness and is the foundation for how we approach our lives.

If you recall, the next goal of survival after simply surviving is maintaining homeostasis. To put it another way, the first goal is to survive, and the second goal is to continue to survive. This is where situational awareness comes into play.

Dr. Mica Endsley, a former chief scientist of the United States Air Force, defines situational awareness as "the perception of the elements in the environment within a volume of time and space."[10] In other words, situational awareness involves our ability to detect and determine what is happening in the world around us. It has a major impact on our ability to maintain homeostasis.

We are bombarded with information all the time. Some of it is undetectable, and some is only detectable by our subconscious. How do we take that information in, parse it successfully, and use it to provide a good outcome? How are we seeing it, whatever "it" is?

Let's use my poor color vision as an example. I don't see the same colors as other people. I have never seen a green tree. They all look brown. So think that through—I don't have green in my world, at least what the consensus has deemed green. I only know this because the doctors have determined that I see the color brown somewhat accurately, so I know that the trees, the

---

[10] Mica Endsley, "Toward a Theory of Situation Awareness in Dynamic Systems," Semantic Scholar, March 1995, https://journals.sagepub.com/doi/10.1518/001872095779049543.

grass, and everything similar look brown to me. When I look at nature, my brown-centric perspective is different than that of a person who can see the color green.

No matter how you receive it, data comes through your five classical senses—sight, sound, smell, taste, touch—and also your sixth sense, which is where you receive information through your subconscious. In fact, I would argue that your subconscious provides your biggest input into your understanding of a situation. It's all a matter of recognizing it: the hair on the back of your neck when it stands up, that feeling you get in the pit of your stomach, or the goosebumps you get when something "feels" off and you can't quite put your finger on it. Unfortunately, we usually write those things off because, as human beings, we mistakenly believe that we and our rational minds are in control of everything.

Fortunately, your subconscious picks up on much more nuance than your conscious mind does. It doesn't understand time or place—it understands events. It understands sensation. Your subconscious can't communicate verbally with you, but it can make you feel different and give you pause to think about what's taking place. It takes a scene that you see through your eyes, hear through your ears, feel on your skin, and smell in your nose and pumps it through your mental database that aligns it all. It lets you know whether things are good, if you should feel nervous, or if you need to be on alert.

Your decision-making process is a four-parter: you absorb and analyze the world of your personal environment and make decisions that lead to your actions in response to what's happening in your world. Without the proper mindset, you are not set up for success. Not having the awareness to detect something coming, analyze the situation, and make a decision may lead to less-than-beneficial actions and your demise. Remember, once you survive the moment, your next goal is to minimize your suffering and finally to live your best possible life, which is also a progression reflected in Maslow's Hierarchy of Needs.

Safety Needs

With your physiological needs mostly taken care of, you can focus on your safety needs. As you move into this level of Maslow's Hierarchy, the assumption is that you have taken care of everything under mindset and situational awareness to survive any immediate problems with massive trauma and homeostasis—the physiological needs.

Safety overlaps with situational awareness in that it further addresses how to identify and manage current and future risks. The distinction is that, at this level, you are no longer thinking in the short term but rather about how to live over the long term: safe, secure, confident, earning a living, creating a home, and finding community.

Now, if you're an overachiever, you may have already read that the next level—Love and Belonging—seems to fit more with community, too. And you're correct. But at this level, "community" involves things like grocery stores, first responders, plumbers, and so forth. These are not your besties. These are resources to help you maintain homeostasis in the long term. The "social standing" Maslow is referring to is your ability to operate within the rules of your community, whatever form that community takes on.

Our safety needs address our need for predictability and stability. We want to feel safe, and safety is all about managing our relationship with risk and, in so doing, managing our relationship with both harm and opportunity.

Maslow describes your safety needs as a need for a safe, orderly, predictable, organized world that can be counted on and in which unexpected, unmanageable, or other dangerous things do not happen. And if they do happen, someone is there to protect you.

I detour slightly from Maslow here, too. I believe that safety is a matter of perspective based on your effective or less-than-effective response to managing risk. So, safety *represents* the security you need to feel in your day-to-day life. The needs themselves, however, are not sufficient to protect you from harm.

When it comes to your safety needs, I do agree with Maslow's statement that "the healthy, normal, fortunate adult in our culture is largely satisfied in his safety needs. Therefore, in a very real sense, he no longer has any safety needs as active motivators." In other words, a civil society typically satisfies a person's physiological and safety needs.

People who take their safety for granted tend to assume their safety will always be provided for without making any real effort and getting input from those who provide that safety. We see proof of this during the aftermath of every disaster; there are accounts of people who thought someone would rescue them. These are hard-learned lessons from the people who ignored or left the responsibility of their safety to others. In doing so, they left themselves unprepared and vulnerable.

Actually, the same can hold true for *all* of our needs. **We become less able to meet our needs if and when we relinquish the responsibility for meeting our needs to others.**

Regarding your safety, society largely operates on a fallacy that television host Mike Rowe is famous for pointing out. It's a lesson he learned on the deck of an Alaskan crab boat while filming an episode of one of his shows.[11]

Crab fishing is a dangerous profession. So, while working—or, as Mike Rowe puts it, trying not to get killed—on the deck of a crab boat, he had an epiphany.

They were out on the Bering Sea when a storm came up, tossing them among thirty-foot waves and chunks of ice. All the while, they were slinging deadly crab pots over the boat, moving ropes—just a lot going on. As the conditions worsened, Mike could see the headlines: *Television Host Drowns in Fishing Boat Accident*. He went to the wheelhouse and asked the captain if he was going to stop work because of the danger. The captain responded, "Safety third."

Mike was confused by his response and replied, "Isn't safety first?"

"The captain's responsibility is not to get the people onboard home alive," he explained to Mike. "It is to get them home. Getting home *alive* is their individual responsibility."

Now, being a captain, if he sees something that's unsafe, he's going to call it out. But ultimately, he is busy piloting the boat.

---

[11] Mike Rowe, "Walk Me through This 'Safety Third' Thing," Mike Rowe, March 24, 2020, https://mikerowe.com/2020/03/walk-me-through-this-safety-third-thing/.

He's trying to get them where the best crabs can be found. Each crew member is responsible for their own survival, so if some clumsy guy gets his foot stuck in a crab pot and is slung eight hundred feet overboard, it's on him, not the captain, to figure out how to survive. Their safety is way down the list of priorities.

After Mike heard that, he headed back out to the pitching deck. This time, he had no illusion about who was responsible for his safety.

How often have we heard "safety first" preached to us? If you go to various workplaces, you'll see signs that say things like "safety is our number one goal," which is basically the "safety first" mantra.

If you are new to preparedness, I am about to shock you: your safety is not everyone's first priority. Nor should it be.

The whole "safety first" cliché essentially means that you put everyone's safety first. So, if I am responsible for your safety, who is responsible for mine? I am assuming someone else will make my safety their top priority, and that's quite a gamble.

We all have unique needs, and the best person to address those needs—especially when it comes to your safety and survival—is you. When you outsource your safety to someone else, you set yourself up for potential failure. Whenever possible, you should take personal responsibility for your safety, security, and preparedness. And if you think about it, this is true for all levels of the Maslow pyramid—if you want to meet your needs and reach your dreams, you have to be your own best advocate.

Love and Belonging

It's time to ascend Maslow's Hierarchy—this time to address your needs regarding love and belonging. In a way, human beings are herd animals. We need to interact with others, belong, and feel love. Our need for satisfying interpersonal relationships usually surfaces when the physiological and safety needs are fairly well met, and our need-driven focus can safely change to family, friends, and acquaintances.

Shelter is a great example of how our needs become more sophisticated as they are met. We require shelter—it is a physiological need. In dire situations, that may consist of a cardboard box or a bunch of sticks and twigs tied together because we need to survive. That would provide protection from the elements until we could figure out our next steps.

When it comes to safety, however, we have moved beyond a shelter—we need a home, and we must earn a living to pay for it. As you pay attention to your need for love and belonging, you may decide you want to share your home with a partner, a spouse, or a dog. When you are squarely concentrating on food and safety, you might sneer at love, claiming that it doesn't matter, but the truth is, we all need love because we all need to connect with others. If we didn't, then solitary confinement wouldn't be a punishment.

If you're still thinking that love and belonging aren't a true need in your life, stay tuned. We'll get to personal honesty later.

Esteem

The fourth tier in Maslow's Hierarchy consists of your need for esteem: self-worth, achievement, and respect from others.

Maslow breaks down esteem into two categories: the esteem you have for yourself and your desire for the respect of others.

Personal esteem relates to your pursuit of achievement, strength, confidence, and the freedom to be your authentic self. At the same time, you have a need for prestige and a reputation based on your perception of the recognition, significance, and appreciation you receive from others. So, you have a need to make yourself awesome, but you also have a need for others to regard you as awesome.

Your esteem needs reveal themselves when shame, self-doubt, and lack of confidence creep into your thoughts, decisions, and actions. That's important to know, especially when it comes to preparedness, because your self-doubt can cause you not to prepare for something or not be as prepared as you are capable of being. It's your self-doubt that hammers your motivation and affects whether you'll work to expand your abilities.

Self-doubt is a little voice in the back of your mind that tells you to take the easy way out of things. It stops many of us from being truly prepared to capitalize on the good in our lives while minimizing the bad; it's the voice that tells us that we don't need to eat right, get fit, or become better at things. Self-doubt minimizes what we think is important and immobilizes us; this is why so many of us in the U.S. opt to sit back, watch YouTube videos, stuff chips in our mouths, and wash it down with a can of chemicals, high-fructose corn syrup, and other unhealthy additions. Self-doubt blows smoke up our asses and convinces us not to be open, honest, and vulnerable with ourselves and with others; it makes us believe that in order for people to like us, we must be less genuine.

When it comes to preparedness, getting in over your head during a dangerous situation, or getting into a dangerous situation at all, is never a good thing. If you don't know how to swim, for example, don't act like you do. If you don't know how to swim, stay the hell out of the water. When it comes to danger, letting your emotional mind overpower your rational mind is the wrong answer. One nonswimmer diving in to save another nonswimmer isn't the right answer.

Self-doubt also matters when you let opportunities slip through your grasp. How many times have we not told someone we love them, and then the day comes when it's too late? We let those opportunities go by. I never said it was easy; in fact, it may be downright difficult.

If your esteem needs are unmet, you might struggle to enjoy the love because you likely will not recognize it when you encounter it.

Self-Actualization

The highest tier in Maslow's Hierarchy is self-actualization. This is about fulfilling your needs of being who you are and knowing what makes you tick. Self-actualization is your need to become the best version of you that you can be, where you follow your dreams.

This is where we hope and try to live to our fullest potential.

Some may balk at the idea of self-actualization being included as a need for preparedness. These are the same individuals who discount self-actualization in favor of focusing solely on survival and safety. At a minimum, they risk never having the opportunity to realize their dreams, and sadly, many don't even know it.

Self-actualization, or the need for it, reveals itself when other needs and levels of needs have been met. The opportunity usually evolves after you successfully meet your lower-level needs.

According to Maslow, only a very small percentage of people self-actualize, so I want to be clear that self-actualizing is not about climbing the corporate ladder or scoring a bunch of real estate deals. Those may be milestones along your path up the pyramid, but in my opinion, they are not the result of self-actualization.

Once upon a time, in a land far, far away, I did the corporate grind and was miserable. If I had continued to run on the rat wheel of corporate America, I would have never figured out how happy I could be living in a trailer in the woods, roaming the country, and being creative. Had I not stripped away all those vestiges of esteem, my growth would have ground to a halt.

In the end, you are not wrong to choose a different path up the pyramid of life. If you want to have the most fulfilling, happy life and be prepared for it, these needs require consideration to get there. This is not about me telling you what to do. I want to give you the tools to figure it out for yourself. As with safety or any of the other levels, don't outsource your self-actualization to anyone, or you'll surely never arrive.

Ultimately, you and you alone are responsible for everything, including living your best possible life. And your journey toward that life begins with mindset.

CHAPTER 3

MINDSET

Like all humans, I have lived a life full of good and bad experiences. When I think back to the outcomes of those experiences, I see how much they were determined by my mindset.

On one hand, a poor mindset led me to believe that spending over a decade in conflict areas wouldn't negatively affect me. Of course, it did—and I attribute being, at times, a bad friend, a difficult family member, and an overall pain in the ass to it. I also attribute many poor decisions and regrettable failures to that initial bad mindset.

On the other hand, a good mindset led to me *only* turning around five times when driving to a six-week stint for PTS (post-traumatic stress) recovery.[12] My good mindset helped me *admit* I was a pain in the ass. My good mindset helped me become

---

[12] Post-traumatic stress results from traumatic experiences—trauma. Therefore, in alignment with how we refer to a fractured leg as an injury, I consider post-traumatic stress an injury, not a disorder. As a result, I do my best to refer to post-traumatic stress as PTS and not PTSD.

a better friend and family member, make better decisions, celebrate awesome outcomes, and experience proud successes.

What Is Mindset?

Mindset is the starting point for how you approach everything in life. It is not necessarily how you think in the moment but rather how your thoughts and thought processes have been influenced by your biases, beliefs, and fears.

In terms of preparedness, mindset is the most important of all the fundamentals because it determines your relationship with reality and how much you allow your perception to shape your perspective of reality. Do you see reality for what it is, or do you manufacture a perceived reality by wrapping it in varying layers of perspective, made up of your learned biases, the impact of the human condition, your culture, and so on?

Your relationship with reality establishes the foundation for all your awareness, and your mindset is the interface you use to determine it. Mindset is your capacity to recognize, understand, and—as much as possible—control how you address the impact of the human condition on your approach to life.

Mindset determines whether:

- you allow bias to influence your understanding and interactions with others and the universe at large
- you find motivation in the face of adversity
- you are honest with yourself when that honesty is uncomfortable and difficult
- you find the grace you are due when you feel you have come up short

What I'm laying out here are not hard and fast rules because today's hard and fast rules become tomorrow's antiquated and outdated rules. Maslow himself revised his theory of human motivation. Now, I'm laying out an evolutionary perspective that represents what others have thought in the past, are thinking in the present, and will think in the future. If we—as individuals and as a species—are to do well and survive in our ever-changing universe, then our thought processes must evolve.

Once you equip yourself with the information presented in this book, it's up to you to determine which parts work best for you and adapt your mindset accordingly. And it will be up to those who follow you over time to do the same.

Human Consciousness

Now that you have the basic overview of mindset, let's dive deeper into human consciousness. Philosopher Evan Thompson states that human consciousness is the starting point for all we are aware of and all we will ever know. It's the sum of our lived experience and is made up of all that is intelligible, thinkable, and observable.[13]

More simply, your consciousness is made up of everything you have experienced, including reading this sentence. As you move forward through this book, the rest of today, tomorrow, and your life, you will add more experiences as they happen—expanding your understanding of everything you've ever encountered, thought, or felt.

---

[13] Evan Thompson, "The Nature of Consciousness: A Neurophenomenological Approach," YouTube, 2017, https://www.youtube.com/watch?v=6K3o-TNJXyM.

Together, all of your experiences happen and reside within your ever-expanding bubble, or what Evan Thompson refers to as the horizon of lived experience, which is the boundary for all of your experiences and understanding. Beyond that boundary lies the unknown and unimaginable, where the thoughts and experiences that you have yet to experience patiently wait to cross your horizon of lived experience and become part of your reality.

As your consciousness is made up of everything that happens within the boundaries of your lived experience, your beliefs, perspectives, and understanding of life experiences come from your lived experience. As you expand your bubble of lived experience, you also increase the amount of information available to help shape your mindset through your experiences. It explains how you use one of life's most effective tools for improving your mindset—your ability to fine-tune your perspective and, in so doing, generate a more accurate understanding of your experiences and beliefs—your version of reality.

That's a critical concept to understand because it means you can intentionally add new and differing experiences and thoughts to your lived experience to improve areas where you may struggle or where you excel, ultimately leading to a more peaceful, happy, and rewarding life.

Some examples of refining perspectives and evolving mindsets are:

- Isaac Newton discovered gravity by searching for the unknown—why does an apple fall from a tree?
- Thomas Edison failed thousands of times before discovering the unknown—how to make the electric light bulb.

- I was able to stop sacrificing friendships, careers, family, and years of happiness to my suicidal case of low self-worth and inflamed, post-traumatic stress-induced self-destruction and instead become the mostly happy, content-with-myself person that I am today.
- A father with a desire to protect his family read this book and used my lived experience to help sharpen his perception of reality.

HUMAN CONSCIOUSNESS

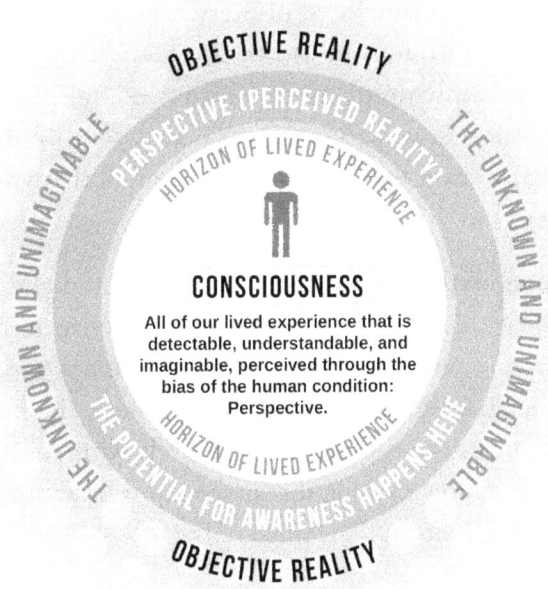

Your human consciousness is responsible for creating the mental pathways you know as mindset. Given that explanation:

- Do you choose to live a prepared, more safe, secure, and confident life?
- Or do you choose to ignore the possibility of future adversity and not take positive, helpful action when you have the opportunity?

Lived Experience

Evan Thompson also states that our lived experience is made up of all that is intelligible, thinkable, and observable. In other words, your consciousness is the sum of your lived experiences and is composed of everything you know, think, and observe. It comprises everything you have consciously and unconsciously done, up to (and including) reading this sentence. Another way to look at it is that your lived experience is the horizon that marks the edge of all that you know and understand.

Therefore, everything you attempt to understand always happens from within your horizon of lived experience. It is the limit of your consciousness, a barrier you cannot pass. However, within your horizon of lived experiences, the boundary of your consciousness expands and travels with you through life and contains everything that makes up your awareness and perception of reality.

Perception and Reality

Understanding perception, reality, and how they relate to us—and us to them—is crucial for navigating a meaningful life. Rarely, if ever, do we see reality for what it is; rather, we usually see reality through our individual lens of perception. Many of us interpret and believe something to be reality when, in fact, it is nothing more than our perception of it, based upon the circumstances of our lived experience: our individual version of the human condition, fraught with all the bias, judgment, and nonsense that we as humans throw onto our reality.

Here are a few examples of the impact of our perception of reality:

- Some people prepare for adversity, while others choose not to prepare despite countless tragic examples of the need to prepare.
- Many people get upset over the opinions of others who don't know them and whose opinions are based on their version of the human condition, which has very little to do with them.
- Each wing of our political albatross believes the impossibility that it is 100% correct and demonizes anyone who believes differently.

As I discussed earlier, our reality only appears within our horizon of lived experience. Only when we experience something consciously or subconsciously does it become part of our lived experience.

However, as it becomes a new addition to our current version of reality, we filter it through our individual understandings of the universe based on everything we've experienced. It's an unavoidable part of the human condition that our less-than-perfect perceptions add up to less-than-perfect perspectives (beliefs).

That becomes a severe problem if your filter of perception is so flawed that it causes your perspective to be way off the baseline of actual reality. For example:

- When I lived a life of constant worry because I believed the hype and was sure the end of the world as we know it was about to happen. The Soviet nuclear threat, Y2K, 9/11, etc., all came and went, and we're still here.
- The times I fell short because doing the right thing and succeeding were unable to overcome my inner selve's low self-worth and the stranglehold it had on me being the best person I could be.
- My lost years spent mired in fear, anger, and disappointment, waiting for the life I wanted to happen rather than enjoying the energy, potential, and satisfaction of struggling to make life happen.

Fortunately, none of us are tied to any of our less-than-perfect perspectives. We can minimize the human condition's biased impact on our understanding and relationship with reality. We can improve our perspective and, in so doing, become the best, most capable versions of ourselves possible.

One guess where to start?

Your mindset.

Everything that follows includes your awareness of what is happening in the universe around you, how you interpret what's happening, the decisions you make based on your interpretations, and the resulting actions you take in response to your awareness. It's garbage in, garbage out if you don't understand that your perspective is nothing more than a version of reality. The truth of the universe happens outside of your lived experience and perception—there is only one reality, and by default, each of us perceives it differently.

Your efforts to more closely align your perspective with objective reality start with understanding that what you are seeing, hearing, and believing is your own perception and then recognizing it as so. If you don't believe you are observing a perspective-skewed reality, then you're never going to get out of the way of biased and inaccurate beliefs. You're just kidding yourself.

Now, maybe you have a very accurate perspective. However, even if it's one degree off from objective reality, it's not true objective reality. Rather, it's skewed by your culture, human condition, bias, and so forth. Therefore, it's still a perspective built on a flawed perception of reality, which is not true reality.

Your goal should be to get your perception of reality as closely aligned with it as possible. Everything you encounter in life comes from within your personal environments, your horizon of lived experience, which dictates your understanding. As you experience life and add to what you know, you do it through that lens. If you are either unaware of your bias or are unable to set it aside, it will skew reality as you go through life, living in a bubble of imperfect, individual perspective.

If you start with a bias at the beginning, you have a faulty premise, and you're only adding to that premise. It's a faulty house of cards based on bad information.

Men and women interpret their lived experiences differently. Then, we add nationalities, cultural experiences, and so on into that mix, and each of us is more likely to develop a different perception and understanding of our world based upon the totality of our individual and unique lived experience.

For example, a person with a deep faith in God is likely to interpret what they encounter in life differently than someone with no belief in God. Even immediate family members who grow up in the same home have differing levels of lived experience and, therefore, differing ways of addressing life.

In other words, we are all a product of our own unique lives of lived experiences, and as such, we all have unique advantages and disadvantages that accompany our individual humanity. At the same time, while we all live in our unique personal environments, our bubbles of consciousness can overlap.

When you share commonalities of lived experience with others, you often have a shared or similar perspective. Your lived experience dictates how you approach the world and interact with others. It sets the stage for how you prepare and respond to the opportunities and struggles that happen within your horizon of lived experience.

Theory of Destruction and Creation

Have you ever considered how you think and how you change your understanding of reality? Not only is it your turn to connect the dots of human consciousness, but it's also your turn

Mindset   49

to deconstruct everything I have said so far and reconstruct it into something better, something new, something more useful, something evolved, that works in your own life. That process is known as the evolution of thought, which is one of the keys—if not *the* key—to preparedness and, ultimately, to achieving the goals of preparedness.

In my opinion, John Boyd is probably the greatest military mind and one of the most consequential thinkers in modern history, even though he was, proudly, a pain in the ass to the military establishment. In his 1976 paper, "Destruction and Creation," Boyd discusses his theory that our evolution of thought occurs through the process bearing the same name.[14] He connects the dots left by mathematician and philosopher Kurt Godel, Nobel-winning physicist Werner Heisenberg, and others to propose that for thought to evolve, we must first deconstruct our current way of thinking about the issue or issues.

I'm a total fan-boy of Boyd. The evolution of thought largely determines how you successfully navigate through a life full of challenges and opportunities in unknown situations. It is a critical aspect of mindset, both individually and collectively. Your thoughts must evolve for you—now and in the future—to not merely survive but thrive in an ever-changing universe.

You can deconstruct your current way of thinking by taking all that you know on the topic or situation and breaking it down into its individual elements. Those individual elements include

---

[14] John Boyd, Destruction and creation , September 3, 1976, https://www.coljohnboyd.com/static/documents/1976-09-03__Boyd_John_R__Destruction_and_Creation.pdf.

not only the factual, objective reality of your understanding but also the incorrect constructs that you, as part of the human condition, add to your understanding. This ultimately influences your perception of the facts.

If you are to effectively expand and evolve your understanding of a topic, issue, or even a random thought, you must analyze these deconstructed parts and then synthesize them to create a new understanding. Lather, rinse, repeat—or risk not surviving. Evolution of thought is essential for us to survive today, tomorrow, and in the generations to come.

There is a lot of buzz around phrases like *your truth*, *my truth*, *your reality*, *my reality*—yet we live in the same reality. We just experience its impact differently. To get as close as possible to the truth—the objective reality—you must strip it down to basic elements and analyze it.

The Dialectic and 360-Degree Preparedness

The opposing forces of Destruction and Creation are known as a dialectic—two opposing points that can both be true and present at the same time. Other dialectical examples are:

- love and hate
- good and evil
- right and wrong
- order and chaos

All of these can be simultaneously true and present. We can love somebody and hate them at the same time. We can simultaneously be confident in our ability to do something and not confident in our chances to be successful in a particular situation.

For example, when the governor of Karbala province in Iraq threatened to have our entire outnumbered and outgunned diplomatic security team executed, I was confident in my ability to handle the thirteen Iraqi military dudes standing across the large room. I knew with certainty, albeit possibly misplaced certainty, that if the situation went south, those dudes in front of me would all be dead. Likewise, I was confident in the ability of each of my teammates to handle their immediate threats.

Despite this, I had zero confidence in our survival lasting much beyond that. After all, we were a team of fifteen Blackwater diplomatic security contractors in a sea of thousands who despised us and wanted to see us die in the most spectacular way possible. So, my dialectic was that while I was highly confident in our abilities, I had zero confidence in our chances. Fortunately, the governor probably realized he would be one of the first to get smoked, so he backed off. And we all went about our business with no one dying that day.

How do Destruction and Creation apply to your mindset and preparedness? Since you only perceive the world through your own rose-colored glasses, your views, and your lived experiences, it's impossible for you to think of everything.

Therefore, when you look at something, it would serve you well to consider the perspective of others and incorporate the relevant part of their perspective into your views. Applying this to security and preparedness, a dialectical perspective—simply put, a "bad-guy perspective"—uses opposing ideas to find a more accurate and precise version of reality by examining your vulnerabilities through the eyes of another.

A dialectical perspective incorporates the knowledge and views of others who think differently so that you may refine and hone your knowledge and views. For example, you secure your home based on your lived experience. A bad guy has a different understanding of how to make your home less secure, so the dialectic is to get inside the bad guy's head to deconstruct how they intend to do it. As a result, you take the lessons you learn and the additional steps necessary to shore up how to make your home even more secure.

You can't predict the future. You can only do your best to understand the bad guy's motivation and course of action in different circumstances—and, as a result, improve your chances of success. The idea is to stay one step ahead of things to better manage life, opportunities, and possibilities.

One of the first things we did in my last Diplomatic Protection training course was plan an attack against a diplomatic security team and the diplomat under our protection. By viewing safety, security, and preparedness through the lens of others who may be intent on harming you or your loved ones, you are essentially applying the same dialectic strategy. This gives you an opportunity to identify strengths and weaknesses in your preparation before you actually need it. That's why the dialectical perspective is so important. It provides you with as much understanding as possible to establish what I call 360-degree preparedness.

Establishing 360-degree preparedness means exactly what it sounds like: you are as prepared as possible for everything you encounter from every direction. We all have a different perspective, so if I can gain some understanding of what those other perspectives are, maybe I can refine my understanding to be better, or maybe I can conclude that someone is full of crap.

Look, it's okay if that's the conclusion I draw—so long as I am being truly honest about my efforts to understand someone. Otherwise, it's just my arrogance, ego, and bias obscuring reality. At the risk of cutting through our own biases, Destruction and Creation are how we gain and improve our understanding.

How to Think Like a Bad Guy

So now that you understand dialectical perspectives, let's take a leap and ask, *How can you think like a bad guy?*

You get into the mindset of a bad guy through the use of Destruction and Creation by

- observing current and past crime trends and methodologies
- breaking those trends and methods down into their fundamental building blocks
- analyzing what fundamentals worked well together and what didn't
- reconfiguring what worked into something new and better—an evolved way of doing things

By following the process of Destruction and Creation, you can continually evolve your understanding so that it is a better fit for your current and future situations. Each experience has the ability to add to your previous understanding and, ultimately, your perspective of the world.

But we're not in this to become a threat, right? This exercise is still valuable because you need to understand other perspectives as much as possible to anticipate—and prepare for—any move they make from any direction at any given time. By understanding how a bad guy thinks, you have the potential to use every experience in a positive way, becoming more prepared and resilient in the process. It also means you never stop learning.

If you are not intentional about your mindset, you can slip into a negative or harmful understanding of yourself, the world around you, and the situations you encounter within your world. Yes, you are entitled to whatever mindset you want, but I vote for a mindset that is not negative or harmful. The other option just sucks, and life is too short and amazing to go through it in a shitty manner.

It is up to each of us to understand and remind ourselves that the only way to maintain a positive and prepared mindset is to be intentional about it. Fortunately, with work, personal honesty, and introspection, you can catch yourself when you're slipping into a negative mindset and shift accordingly.

It's Not Push-Button Technology

Now, you can't just push a button and change your mindset. That's not what I'm suggesting here. What I am saying, however, is that there is a process, through life experience, to change, fine-tune, and exercise an improved mindset.

If you're in a bad mood, you can't always just snap yourself out of it—oftentimes, you have to work hard at it. As a sufferer of PTS, I now know that, by default, my mindset wants to protect me. My subconscious is constantly examining the world, looking for threats and waiting to signal me through uncomfortable sensations in my body.

When I receive those alert sensations of fear and anxiousness, it's my subconscious that, based on past experiences, feels threatened by something that's going on around me, no matter how ridiculous that fear may seem in the present. The sensations I receive may include nervousness, depression, anxiety, and so on, up a sliding scale of intensity.

To minimize the discomfort, I have to figure out why I am experiencing certain feelings and determine whether they are legitimate or simply my subconscious trying to protect me from nothing more than memories. Since most people aren't trying to hurt me, it's the latter, and I thank it for trying to protect me but reassure it and myself that we're okay.

Does it always work? No, but as I go about my day, I work to create and maintain an intentional mindset and avoid slipping into negativity. It doesn't just happen—it takes practice and effort. My years of practice have taught me that if we work at it, we can arrive at a place in life where we will be better prepared to understand and more effectively interact with our mindset. As a result, when we need a mental shift, we'll be much more capable and in control.

What About Self-Control?

So, if you have the ability to change your mindset and values that keep your dialectical thinking in check, what role does self-control play in mindset so that you ultimately use your powers for good? Or, at the very least, how do you minimize negatives and maximize positives?

First of all, if you try to analyze everything as a potential threat like I did when my PTS was at its worst, you will drive yourself nuts. That's not the point. But you do want to pause and analyze why certain things make you feel good, and other things and situations within your personal environment make you uncomfortable. Then, every time you have a new sensation or experience in life, you likewise have an expanded horizon of lived experience.

Your self-control starts with a self-examination of your mind. Are you reacting appropriately or inappropriately? Are you behaving like a person who is being attacked or like someone who is overreacting to a knucklehead making a lane change closer than you'd prefer?

When you're not in right alignment with reality, a PTS-riddled person such as myself may feel that nearly every minor glitch and driving error from our fellow commuters, regardless of whether it's true or not, is a personal attack trying to kill or maim me. As a result, I can lose my shit in the cab of my truck, screaming, "That dude tried to kill me!"—not because I was really in danger, but because he violated my safe driving standard.

Unfortunately for me, those minor traffic glitches when someone does something in a manner that is less safe than I approve of are perceived by my subconscious as an attack. It's my subconscious, out of fear and a desire to protect myself, that then injects a central nervous system full of fear response along with the physical sensations of being attacked. The physical sensations escalate from mild nervousness along a baseline of fear directly to anxiousness, anger, panic, and doom. And in response, I'd have a total PTS meltdown in the cab of my truck.

When not in right alignment with reality, as was the case when I was deep in my post-traumatic stress, my subconscious would incorrectly perceive a routine day in traffic as a series of attacks and typically involved a five-step process.

1. Prep for my drive through what my brain believed to be—and made me feel similar to—a trip through downtown Baghdad, just waiting for an attack.
2. When the perceived attack happens (someone merges into my lane), I respond by going nuclear in my truck.
3. Blame the other driver for the situation and, in so doing, justify my rage and lack of control.
4. Speed up and get primed to do it all again by screaming at the next person who "tries to kill" me.
5. Head into the rest of my day pissed off and fired up.

When in a closer relationship and right alignment with reality, as is mostly the case now, my subconscious correctly perceives a routine day in traffic as a series of normal driving near misses and also involves a five-step process.

1. I cope ahead before starting my truck by reminding myself with intent that I am home in the U.S. and that any near misses are not an ambush that needs a war-zone-level response.
2. Instead of going nuclear when someone does something unsafe, I take a breath, a tactical pause, and recognize the situation for what it truly is—people make mistakes and do dumb things when driving.
3. Mentally congratulate myself for not losing my shit while mentally wishing the other driver a great day with no more traffic goof-ups.
4. Safely slow down or speed up to create time and distance between myself and the glitching driver.
5. Head into the rest of my day in a good mood and ready to enjoy life.

We all have a choice. The more honest we are with ourselves, the better we will understand perception versus reality and exercise self-control. Your self-control (and practicing it when times are not as cataclysmic as your subconscious believes) will prepare you for the times when the situation *is* as urgent as your subconscious believes. In short, giving in to the habit of reacting badly to situations when times are not hard will likely set you up for failure when times are hard. Self-control, it's a thing!

When we talk about preparedness, survival, safety, and self, we are contemplating some very emotional topics. Appropriately responding to your preparedness requires self-control when asking and coming to terms with, *"What are you truly preparing for?"*

In the end, this is not a book that will answer that question for you; it's a book that equips you to answer it for yourself. I'm not telling you to prepare for nuclear war, famine, or a super volcano—those are boogeymen that rightly or wrongly live in your head—but do take inventory of your emotions and determine if your preparedness is appropriate or an overreaction to a remote or impossible possibility.

Is It Perception or Reality?

By being dialectical and practicing Destruction and Creation with yourself, you will be better prepared to make sound decisions based more on reality than subjective perspective. With that, the way you approach your life and preparedness has to be based on personal honesty, or you will build your life on the faulty foundation of believing your own nonsense.

Next, check in with yourself by asking:

- Have I honestly put my biases into check?
- What worries me, why, and is it justified?
- Whatever my bogeymen are, am I being personally honest about my response to them?

A lot of preppers, like myself, want to prepare for the end of the world. Look, I'm being personally honest here. I've got beans, bullets, bandages, and batteries. I have stockpiles of other stuff too. But at some point, I had to ask myself:

- *When was the last time the human race went extinct?* Hint: Despite ourselves, we're still here.

- *How likely is it that the world will end tomorrow?* If I'm being honest, it's most likely that the world's not going to end in my lifetime.
- So finally, I had to ask myself: *Do I really need to prepare for the world to end, or do I just need to prepare enough to survive another problem in a long line of problems that humans face on a regular and recurring basis?*

Your answer comes down to personal honesty and the perspective of having the dialectics and willingness yourself. In the end, the only way we can get our mindset where it needs to be is to call ourselves out on our own bullshit. As a result, you and you alone are responsible for your actions, reactions, and inactions. You are not responsible for what other people do. Remember, "Safety third."

Lastly, always remember it's through Destruction and Creation that you can improve the accuracy of your beliefs and align closer with reality. Every little data point of experience you gain contributes to the beliefs you develop over time, which will influence your mindset and outcome.

In the next chapter, we will consider how bias plays into the equation. While we may be more resistant to considering the possibility that our current beliefs might be wrong, it's a good idea, when in doubt, to check in and make sure we are present and effective in our thought process. *Mindset first!*

CHAPTER 4

BIAS—THE LINE BETWEEN PERSPECTIVE AND REALITY

"**D**RIVE! DRIVE! DRIVE!" I screamed.

"Fuck!" We were rolling right up and onto the "X." The spot where the three white-clad bad guys had set up and were ready to launch their deadly attack.

I could see in their eyes that these dudes came to fight. They were tall and lean and looked exactly like you'd expect people to look after spending years fighting against and surviving the total weight of the U.S. Military.

All three were perfectly positioned off the street and behind the cover of a parked van. They were covered head to toe in a pale white, and weirdly, everything they carried, even their weapons, was pale white.

Two AKs and an RPG![15]

---

[15] Rocket-propelled grenade

We're going to eat that RPG!

We needed to do something fast, and it had to happen now. So, sitting in the right front passenger seat, the vehicle commander's seat, I began pounding my fist on the dash and screaming for my driver to "DRIVE!"

My driver, likewise reacting to the blast of fear-induced adrenaline, smashed the accelerator, passed the van, ran the stop sign, and did as all good high-threat motorcade drivers did in 2007 Iraq, "drive through—push through—ram through," and got us off the "X" without taking a round.

Unfortunately, my driver wasn't my driver. She was my girlfriend. She was my girlfriend who, tired of never leaving our Las Vegas safe haven, a.k.a. home, had planned a nice early dinner for us at a swanky restaurant near the Las Vegas Strip.

It was an early dinner to work around her boyfriend's (my) problems at the time with crowds, lights, noises, and anything else that could possibly trigger me. And while our 4 p.m. dinner started fantastically, my desire to give my girlfriend one decent night out caused me to overstay my post-traumatic-stress-issued party pass.

As the evening moved forward, so too did my reaction to what my brain perceived as threats. The people, the noises, and the lights took me from my standard protective measure of putting my back against the wall in a reasonably safe restaurant section to a paranoia-driven hallucination of bad guys trying to kill me.

While my hallucinations may be extreme examples of paranoia, they show how quickly our minds can make the easy jump from protective to paranoid. Protective involves effectively managing risk. Paranoid involves ineffectively managing risk.

Protective responses to risk are measured and rational based on the current facts. Paranoid responses, on the other hand, are not aligned with the facts and are instead based on cognitive bias, the human condition, and, ultimately, perception.

Protective—good. Paranoid—not so good.

In this chapter, we're going to look at the impact bias has on mindset. Before we move on to the other fundamentals of preparedness, it's imperative to understand how we think so we can make the best decisions possible and set ourselves up for success in every area of life.

What Is Cognitive Bias?

The Cambridge Dictionary defines cognitive bias as "the way a particular person understands events, facts, and other people, which is based on their own particular set of beliefs and experiences, and may not be reasonable or accurate."[16]

My definition of bias: *when people who don't know anything have the highest level of confidence in what they think they know.* When people realize that they don't know as much as they think they do, their confidence diminishes. As they learn more and more, over time, their confidence rebuilds in a different way (hopefully, one that is positive).

---

[16] "Cognitive Bias Definition | Cambridge English Dictionary," Cambridge Dictionary, accessed August 11, 2024, https://dictionary.cambridge.org/us/dictionary/english/cognitive-bias.

To figure out what constitutes bias and perhaps identify a few of your own, let's stick with the Cambridge definition for now, starting with the first half: "the way a particular person understands events, facts, and other people." That is perception. Cognitive bias, therefore, is rooted in a person's perception.

I want to differentiate between perception and perspective because that will factor into the second half of the Cambridge definition. As discussed earlier, perspective is how you feel and believe about something. Therefore, while perception is how you think and understand, perspective is your point of view and what you feel about things.

In other words, the *way* you think determines *what* you think. Your perception gives birth to and fosters your perspective. When it comes to mindset, those are important distinctions to understand.

Biases are part of the human condition that can creep into your judgment, outlook, and perspective and affect your preparedness. If you are too confident in your preparedness, you may find that it is a house of cards built upon a San Andreas-sized fault, and it is ready to crumble—you just don't know it.

Remember, it didn't go so well for the first two little pigs; houses made of straw and sticks didn't stop the Big Bad Wolf. *What's your house made of?*

How and Where Biases Develop

Sometimes, our perception and perspective are fairly accurate, but biases make them less so. And we are usually not fans of finding out we're wrong. Our perceptions make us unique, and individual experience happens to all of us.

Even when a group of people are all participating in a collective experience, such as a baseball game, each person's experience is unique to them. Not only do players experience the game differently than the fans, but the fans on one side of the ball field experience the game differently than the fans on the other. Likewise, everyone interprets their experience differently because their interpretation of this group experience will be based on their lifetime of individually lived experiences.

Our experiences also vary geographically. Here in the U.S. alone, someone who grew up in Maine or Alaska will have a very different experience than those who grew up in Florida or Hawaii. Looking within the state of Florida, someone who grew up in the Florida panhandle would have a very different childhood experience than someone who grew up in Miami. We could even get down to the neighborhood or individual household level on different experiences—dividing people further by culture, DNA, and so on. My experience growing up in Northeast Los Angeles during the 1970s and 1980s was very different from a kid growing up in Compton, twenty miles away.

Remembering that perception gives birth to perspective, you only gain your perspective as you have experiences in life. That's why you have a tight bond with your beliefs—they are developed and nurtured over time. You have a tight bond with your experiences as well; you have an *emotional* bond with your beliefs, which can cause angst if they are questioned.

Cognitive bias is a person's fallible perception of the accuracy of their beliefs, which they often think are infallible. As you learn, you experience sensations that make you paranoid, and that is to be expected. You are designed to do that, but you are not intended to stay there. You don't know what you don't know, but you should be finding out. If the goal is to align your perceptions and perspectives with the true reality of a situation (objective reality) as much as possible, you can protect yourself without living in a state of paranoia. Every little step is a step forward—which is progress. The sensations that trigger your reaction do not mean you have to give in to the temptation to react disproportionately.

As I mentioned, my color vision sucks. I'm also a Valley dude who grew up as a Southern California Dungeons & Dragons-playing surfer kid. Therefore, I perceive things differently than you. And you perceive things differently than others. It's those perceptions that create our unique perspectives.

Perception and perspective are two factors you can use to better understand reality. If you subtract your perceptions from your perspective, the result is the true reality of your situation:

Perspective - Perception = Objective Reality

Why is that important to preparedness? Because when we can admit that we may not understand the situation for what it truly is, we can work to identify areas of our perception that may be wrong.

Think about how safety and security are handled; you work to minimize the threats to you. If you identify incorrect perceptions, you can either correct them, minimize them, or work to eliminate them from your perspective altogether and move closer to the baseline of objective reality.

Isn't Perception the Same as Reality?

Unique experiences are part of the human condition, so are cognitive biases. The range between reality and your perspective is measured by your perception, so you can work to eliminate as much error-based perception as possible from your perspective.

Since we already know there is a margin of error in our perspectives, we should assume that there will be times when we need to examine and reexamine our beliefs. Perception is not reality—rather, it's our limited knowledge of reality. The goal is to align it as close as possible to objective reality.

It is only by admitting that any amount of perspective is a variance from true or objective reality that you truly open the possibility of honestly addressing the degree of separation between reality and your perspective. That area is filled with your unique perception and influenced by your cognitive biases. If your perspective contains cognitive bias—which we know to be fallible—you must do your best to minimize its impact to truly be prepared.

Now that you know that cognitive bias skews your perspective from the objective reality baseline and affects your ability to achieve the goals of preparedness, what can you do about it? You need to learn how you learn. Once you grasp the stages of learning, you can better understand where your biases exist.

Four Stages of Learning

When it comes to learning, my friend, retired Force Recon Marine and president of Exlog Global, George Taylor, teaches that humans go through four general stages:

- Unconscious incompetence
- Conscious incompetence
- Conscious competence
- Unconscious competence

Visualize a line with unconscious incompetence at one end and unconscious competence at the other. To improve, you must walk through all four learning stages.

Unconscious incompetence is the starting point, where you don't know what you don't know on a topic or skill. You are so unknowledgeable about and unskilled in whatever you are interested in, you're too ignorant to understand it. You may not even know what it is. You may not even know whether it exists.

During this stage, people do things wrong—or possibly right—without knowing why they are right or wrong—or even whether what they did was wrong or right. They don't have the context to know either way. It's education through trial and error.

The quest for self-improvement enables you to progress from unconscious incompetence to conscious incompetence. When I first started playing rugby, I thought, *How hard can it be?* After all, I was an Army Ranger who loved smashing into things. *It should be easy*, I thought. And it was—until my first game.

When I picked up the ball, took a few steps, and got clobbered, unaware of how to handle a rugby ball, I hit the ground and popped my rib cage. It turns out rugby is a different beast than American football, and I needed to learn how to play it better. Who knew? Right then, I went from unconscious incompetence to conscious incompetence.

Conscious incompetence is the second stage of learning, where you begin to get a general idea about whatever you are trying to do or understand. This is a stage of incompetence where you understand enough that you don't really know what you're doing or attempting to understand.

After feeling my ribs pop, leaving my lungs somewhere on the ground, and hearing my championship-winning rugby coach, Jim Muldoon, yell, "Get up, you dozy bastard!" it's fair to say I was consciously incompetent—made aware of how little I actually knew about playing rugby—at that moment. I knew I had to work if I was going to keep enjoying the free beer and smashing into people while being consciously incompetent. It isn't fun when we realize we suck at something—so we either give it up or keep going to get rid of our suckitude.

Now, conscious competence is the learning stage in which you become adept at whatever you're learning. You still have to think about it, but you understand it more and more. Continuing with my short-lived, free-beer rugby career as an illustration, I kept working at it until I could see the hit coming and make the conscious decision to secure the ball in a way that works for rugby and not in a way that works for American football. It took a few weeks of sucking wind and a trip to the emergency room, but eventually, I improved. Conscious competence happens over time with experience.

Unconscious competence is the nirvana of doing things well when you can make things happen without thinking about it. Continuing with my rugby illustration, when I learned how to tuck the ball away and get smashed properly, I was unconsciously competent. When you are unconsciously competent, you instinctively know what needs to be done and how to get it done.

Unconscious competence is where you want to be when it comes to succeeding in living your best life, but your biases can get in the way. Now that you know the four stages of learning, my personal definition of bias makes a little more sense: *when people who don't know anything have the highest level of confidence in what they think they know.*

Learning allows you to minimize the negative and promote the positive. Three big cognitive biases can skew your perspectives regarding preparedness: the Dunning-Kruger Effect, Normalcy Bias, and Confirmation Bias. These biases distort your reality and negatively impact your preparedness. Let's look at these and then get personally honest about them.

Dunning-Kruger Effect

The Dunning-Kruger effect is based on the work of David Dunning and Justin Kruger.[17] It is a theory that establishes a relationship between a person's knowledge and experience on a topic or situation and their confidence in dealing with that

---

[17] David Dunning, "The Dunning–Kruger Effect: On Being Ignorant of One's Own Ignorance," Science Direct, June 7, 2011, https://www.sciencedirect.com/science/article/abs/pii/B9780123855220000056?via%3Dihub.

topic or situation. Dunning-Kruger's concept proposes that people believe they are more capable than they are—they think they are great when it comes to doing or thinking things.

THE DUNNING-KRUGER EFFECT

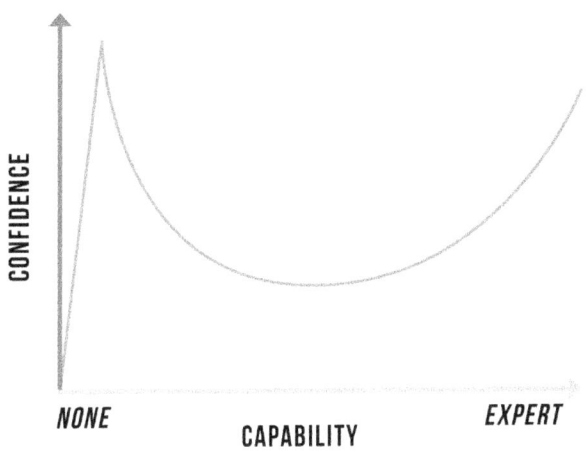

The Dunning-Kruger effect, then, describes an explanation and measure of one's overconfidence. History has repeatedly shown us that overconfidence is responsible for many heartaches and tragedies. It only makes sense in hindsight when looking back at unconscious incompetence.

The Dunning-Kruger effect kicks in when someone gains a small bit of knowledge, experience, or understanding to the point that they suddenly obtain a large, unrealistic amount of confidence in whatever it is. In short, they suddenly become a know-it-all and try to project that. At this stage, they believe they are vastly more capable than they really are.

Unfortunately, that flavor of overconfidence can derail a person or situation versus actual preparedness. Fortunately, the harmful end of the Dunning-Kruger effect may not last long because, as people gain more knowledge, many learn enough to realize they are not as good as they thought when they had very little knowledge.

In time, their level of confidence becomes more aligned with their level of understanding and ability. However, Dunning-Kruger research posits that, regardless of a person's achieved skill and understanding, even at their peak, they will never have the level of confidence that they did when they were unconsciously incompetent.

Normalcy Bias

We always want things to be normal, right? So, you might look at your circumstances or a particular situation and deduce that it's not so bad. Normalcy bias often leads people to underestimate the potential impact or implication of a situation—especially if it's an impending disaster type of situation—to the extent that they may completely deny it.

Normalcy bias causes many not to prepare at all because they believe, "That won't happen to me."

We want things to be normal because normal is safe. If you were safe one minute ago and everything stayed normal, then you want to keep on that trajectory because that means things will continue to remain normal. In time, you create a narrative in your head—so committed to normalcy that you're actually off the reality baseline. Again, it comes down to perception.

Normalcy bias is a spectrum, not an all-or-nothing. While it may keep some from preparing at all, it may also cause others to only partially prepare—neither option is optimal. If you are reading this book, you're at an advantage regarding normalcy bias—just by reading a book on preparedness, you recognize on some level that you need to prepare. I'm willing to wager that you have a better handle on your normalcy bias than the unprepared and unconcerned.

Confirmation Bias

Confirmation bias is a cognitive bias that causes people to favor information that confirms their preexisting beliefs, and they seek this information out almost exclusively.[18] One scroll through the algorithmic world of social media confirms the confirmation bias, right?

This can lead people to ignore evidence that contradicts or challenges their beliefs and, instead, watch sources that align with their perspective. In many cases, we can no longer call it "news" because it has more in common with siloed sources and echo chambers that only say what their readers, viewers, and listeners want to hear, read, see, etc.

Confirmation bias can cause major problems with your perspective. It is a vast disservice to your decision-making process when you only take in the information you agree with. Confirmation bias reduces your ability to think individually

---

[18] Raymond S. Nickerson, "Confirmation Bias: A Ubiquitous Phenomenon in Many Guises," Sage Journals, June 1998, https://journals.sagepub.com/doi/10.1037/1089-2680.2.2.175.

and uniquely; rather, it can lead to a dangerous tribal-like mentality.

When summarized, confirmation bias equates to garbage in, garbage out. Limited sources of limited information result in limited quality decisions. When you're only given half of the information, at best, you'll only be half-prepared.

Overcoming Cognitive Biases

We already know that, as humans, we cannot eliminate our biases completely. Therefore, to achieve our goals of preparedness, we must work to minimize them.

I have found that when I'm struggling or facing a dilemma, reminding myself that I may always be at least *partially* wrong provides me room for improvement. This reminder allows me to do things better, get better, and have a better life.

Your improvement exists in refining and sharpening your perspective. Ask yourself:

- What if I'm wrong?
- What if I'm only partially right?
- What if there is an opportunity I'm missing?
- What is that opportunity?

Your willingness to question yourself and your beliefs and perspectives can work to minimize the impact of your cognitive biases on yourself and your preparedness.

From there, a little Destruction and Creation can give you a perspective on your biases and how you look at the world.

Using Boyd's theory, you can take the definition of cognitive bias, break it down into its parts, and synthesize it into something beneficial.

It Still Begins with Mindset

We learned in the last chapter that when it comes to preparedness, mindset is the starting point for everything that follows. Without a proper mindset—which also means being willing to question yourself, question things, and question others to try to make yourself better—you will struggle to meet the goals of preparedness. You may survive, but you will always have unwanted struggle.

No one is right all the time. The crazy thing is that while not everyone will have a correct opinion on every topic, they will *perceive* that their opinion is correct on every topic they believe in—until they become aware that their opinion is incorrect.

Regardless, a person believes they are right until they know they are not—and are willing to acknowledge, accept, and admit it. That, my friends, is called evolution and growth, which are critical to minimizing your biases, fine-tuning your mindset, and enhancing your situational awareness skills, which lead to living your best-prepared life.

CHAPTER 5

SITUATIONAL AWARENESS AND DECISION-MAKING

When I was a kid, I was hit by a car while riding my bike to school, right at the corner of our playground. At the time, I attended a Catholic grammar school about six blocks from home and had to cross a blind alley to get there. An old brick building stretched to the corner, but crossing the alley was a good route to get to school quickly—so long as you were paying attention.

Now, I should mention that my mother gave me two dollars each morning for my lunch. And I figured out that I could eat for one dollar and spend the rest at the 7-Eleven on the corner, where they had video games and porn magazines. I played video games every morning before school, and while they would never sell me any porn, it wasn't a store that the uptight nuns approved of.

On this particular morning, after battling hordes of Space Invaders, I had just a few minutes to get to school. And, because I was in a rush, I didn't look around the corner of the brick building as I darted into the alley, which is how I got hit. While it didn't vaporize me like a Space Invader, it did send me flying, leaving my bike a bent mess underneath the car. Thankfully, I wasn't hurt, but that didn't mean I avoided any consequences. A fellow student and our principal, Sister Ramona, made sure of that.

After getting to school, I was called into the principal's office, where Sister Ramona didn't give two shits about me getting hit by the car. A fellow student ratted me out, and it was the fact that I was slaughtering virtual aliens in an establishment that also sold pornography that did not settle well with her.

Had I been situationally aware enough to look around the corner before blasting into the alley, I would have never gotten hit, caught, or into trouble. My fellow student wouldn't have snitched on me to Sister Ramona for going to 7-Eleven, where they had *PLAYBOY* magazines. Do you want to bet that I never made that mistake again? I never again rode my bike out into the street or an alley without stopping and leaning over the handlebars to see if a car was coming—not to mention the second-order effects of the nuns and the third-order effects from my mother when she found out I was killing aliens rather than eating steamed hot dogs and soggy buns.

What Is Situational Awareness?

Situational awareness refers to your ability to detect and understand what's happening in the world around you, now and in the future. The information you gain feeds into the decisions you make about current and future possibilities, which in turn leads to the actions you take.

After mindset, situational awareness—some call it "SA" for short—is the next most critical preparedness fundamental. Situational awareness is consciously and unconsciously observing the world around you, receiving information from those observations, and interpreting that information so that you can load the data into your decision-making process as needed. Basically, you see, hear, or learn something, then run it through your mind's filters to understand it.

Once you understand the situation, you are prepared to make a decision based on the information you gathered. Situational awareness could lead you to decide that you need to be at the airport earlier because the last time you traveled, you were late and missed your flight. Or, it could be, "Hey, that bus is about to jump the curb and head straight for me. What do I do to stay safe?"

Your awareness-based decisions lead to action. The things you do or don't do eventually lead to your successes and failures. There is no specific timeline for situational awareness; it can happen in an instant, a few seconds, several minutes, or even longer.

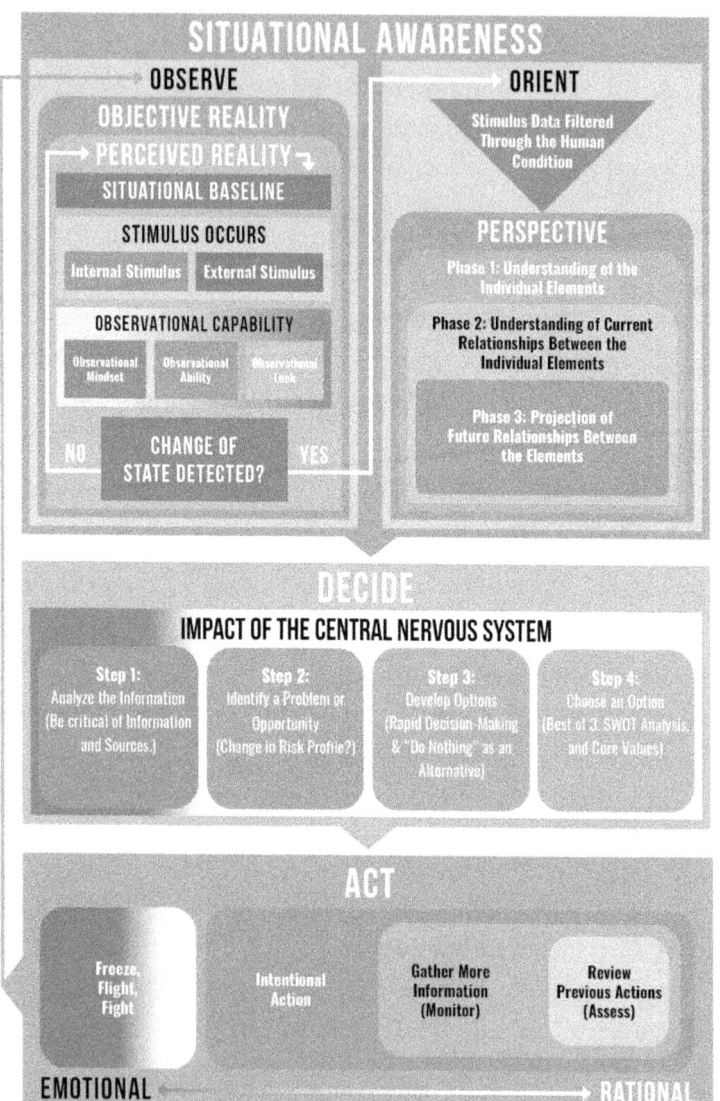

Understanding the process is important so that as your need for awareness ebbs and flows, you can scale the fundamental building blocks of your awareness accordingly.

With that, the process introduced in this chapter breaks down the fundamental order of your situational awareness, decision-making, and action-taking. This is where you learn how to refine your thought process to increase your capability to mitigate threats and seize opportunities.

The OODA Loop

In addition to his theory on Destruction and Creation, John Boyd created the decision-making model known as the OODA Loop, which stands for Observe, Orient, Decide, and Act. The OODA Loop provides a concise explanation of situational awareness and, when broken down, gives you a firmer grasp of the process you go through to attain it.

One of my best friends, Del, who introduced me to the OODA Loop, likes to remind people that the first two phases of the OODA Loop, Observe and Orient, make up your situational awareness, with Decide (decision-making) and Act (taking action) following in succession.

The individual phases of the OODA Loop can be defined as follows:

- **Observe:** This is the process of using your six senses to observe the world around you and your personal environment and detect what's happening within it. The output of what you detect through your senses leads you from the observe to the orient phase.

- **Orient:** The orient phase is when you decide what you do with the information/data detected through your observations. During the orient phase, you analyze and prioritize the data you receive from your observations. It is also during the orient phase that perspective comes into play by applying or removing biases and factors of the human condition.

- **Decide:** Once you have parsed your observed information during the orient phase, it's time to make a good or bad, voluntary or involuntary decision about a potential course of action. There is a saying that "it's never the action you take that's the problem; it's always the decision you make right before taking the action that's the problem." That applies here.

- **Act:** Last, the output of your decision-making process is putting your decisions into action.

My Mind4Survival process is founded on Boyd's OODA Loop while incorporating Endsley's definition of situational awareness, Jeff Cooper's Color Code, and other commonly accepted theories. My Mind4Survival formula, however, drills down and illustrates what is taking place within each phase of the OODA Loop, tying it all together. As such, it is broken down further and resynthesized (Destruction and Creation) based on my life within my horizon of lived experience—which, as we know, is my perspective.

Even though we'll swim in Boyd's Observe and Orient lanes for the all-too-important situational awareness portion of this chapter, we will follow through into the decision-making and action-taking phases as well.

That's important to understand for two reasons. First, if your observation and orientation are off, your decisions and subsequent actions may similarly be off and increase your likelihood of experiencing a less-than-favorable situational outcome. Again, garbage in, garbage out.

Second, when you find yourself stuck in the moment and unable to think your way through a situation, you'll be able to fall back on this system, walk yourself through it, and know exactly where you are so you may find out what the holdup is in making a decision and/or taking action. Then, you'll be better prepared to hone in more quickly and accurately where you need to in your OODA Loop and work your way through the decision-making process to set yourself up to take the most effective action possible.

For this reason, I will also address the remaining components of the OODA Loop: Decision and Action. To be clear, situational awareness is *not* the entire OODA Loop decision-making process. Rather, situational awareness is the observe and orient phases of the decision-making process. Your motivation for becoming situationally aware is to *move toward* and increasingly feed your decision-making process with as much valid objective-based information as possible while minimizing as much subjective, reality-altering perspective as possible.

Observe: Objective Reality and Perception

Looking at the Mind4Survival Decision-Making Process diagram, I'll start by breaking down Boyd's Observe phase. The Observe phase is where you have the opportunity to perceive the true reality of your personal environment. This is where you take in everything possible through your senses. Do you see, hear, smell, taste, or sense something?

When it comes to the accuracy of perception, I believe that the accuracy and inaccuracy of each of our perceptions follow the bell curve. Individually, some perceptions are 100 percent correct, some are 100 percent wrong, and most fall somewhere in between on the bell curve. In the end, none of us are right or wrong 100 percent of the time, and quite often we are partially right and partially wrong. And, on the partially wrong side of things lives the playground of opportunity for self-improvement and refinement.

Because it's so important, I must reiterate that *there is always one, and only one, true objective reality.* While your perception may be close to objective reality, it is always open to the potential of having at least one degree of separation from the reality baseline due to the uniqueness of the human condition and each of us as individuals.

So why is all of that important?

Ultimately, by holding your observations as close to true reality as possible, you can build the best possible foundation for making the most accurate decisions possible.

That's essential when it comes to survival, safety, and self.

Observe: Situational Baseline

Starting with the Observe phase, you begin with your situational baseline. Your situational baseline is the situational homeostasis of your personal environment. It's the level norm of feeling that is in alignment with Maslow's deficiency and growth needs. Because you know that the situation is safe enough right now to read this book comfortably, the situational baseline of your personal environment is one that, if it remains the same one minute to the next, will be as safe as it was when we started. When that's the case, and your reality baseline remains unchanged, without introducing any new stimuli, you will continue to feel safe and comfortable.

However, when change happens within your personal environment, it creates stimuli that, if detected through your observations, inform you that there has been a shift in your situational baseline. Whether the shift in your baseline is good, bad, or indifferent does not matter. What matters is that you detect the change in the baseline of your situational homeostasis. Without detection, your capability to mitigate threats and capitalize on opportunities may never occur, meaning you are more vulnerable to less desirable outcomes.

As a result, you monitor your current environment for any stimulus that indicates a change to your baseline, causing you to think about something outside of your current state.

At your most basic, you are an individual element amongst other individual elements within your personal environment. By monitoring the individual elements, you are likewise monitoring for any of their individual shifts in the baselines of your personal environment.

Therefore, just because something affects your situational baseline doesn't mean it's harmful. Again, suppose you're reading a book or listening to music and likely not worrying about how safe you feel. In that case, that's because the baseline of your situational homeostasis is constant: *If I was safe and secure two seconds ago, and nothing has changed, I should be safe and secure right now. As long as nothing changes, I'll stay that way.* As a result, you can enjoy your music, a glass of wine, and a quiet moment without constantly worrying about "what-if" problems.

Our struggle with observing, however, is that we must be capable of detecting shifts in our baseline to be able to observe and orient to what is causing the shift. As you learned with the success formula, your success depends on your capability to detect shifts in the baseline and is therefore dependent upon your mindset, ability, and luck. The downside is that you do not always have the mindset, ability, or luck to detect a change in the state of your personal environment.

Therefore, while there may be a shift, your perception of your situational baseline remains the same because you did not detect it. Subsequently, despite the change within your personal environment, your perceived baseline will remain unchanged until a stimulus within your objective reality creates a detectable change of state. Otherwise, what happens is similar to not noticing a stranger who walks up behind you. While they are real, they are not part of your perceived reality until you detect their presence.

There are two ways to detect any stimulus that occurs: externally and internally.

External stimuli—what you see, feel, hear, smell, and taste—are received through your conscious mind. Internal stimuli, on the other hand, are received through your subconscious mind.

An easy way to explain this is that you can detect external stimuli through your five classical senses:

- Do you see something?
- Do you hear something?
- Do you smell, feel, or taste something that would tell you there is a change in the baseline of your situation?

Your internal "sixth-sense" stimulus results from your subconscious detecting a change of state within your personal environment. As a result, when your subconscious mind detects a change in your situational baseline that your conscious mind does not detect, your subconscious alerts you from within your body by creating and prompting you with sensations that are outside of your body's normal homeostatic baseline. My experience with monitoring my body's internally manifested sensations is that they fill a bell curve between total fear of a threat and overexuberance from an unrealistic and opposite perspective.

When it comes to threat signaling, your "sixth-sense" sensations manifest themselves as sensations-vibrations-feelings within your body. Those sensations, depending upon the perceived severity of the threat, scale up in intensity along a spectrum of worry and fear-based discomfort and unease. They do everything from making the hair on the back of my neck stand up to causing sensations of apprehension, depression, anxiety, dread, pain, etc. In effect, when my subconscious, correctly or incorrectly, perceives there to be an ongoing or future problem, especially concerning my safety and security, it sets off alarms from within my body.

Similarly, when my subconscious detects a possible opportunity, it will often create good feeling sensations from within my body. Those good sensations manifest themselves along a bell curve, running from slightly comfortable to euphoric.

The challenge with your sixth-sense sensations is your ability to interpret them correctly. While extremely powerful in their ability to grab your attention through internal body-prompted, sixth-sense sensations, your subconscious doesn't always get it right. In effect, to keep you safe from threats and maximize opportunity, your subconscious alerts you through body sensations based on any number of touchstone events in your life.

Your subconscious never takes a break—it's on 24/7/365. Even when your conscious mind is taking a break through sleep, daydreaming, or inattentiveness, your subconscious typically continues working to inform and protect you. Your subconscious loves to try to protect you by using the fundamental building blocks of past good and bad experiences to project on current and future events.

Your subconscious ties together past significant touchstone experiences with the individual elements that were present during the event. For example, let's assume something traumatic occurred on a hot summer day—a small red car was involved, and you were in the desert. Afterward, even years later, your subconscious may begin alerting you when those elements begin to show up in your present day.

Using myself as an example, after years spent in dangerous and hot climates, my subconscious, as the heat rises, will create a sensation of nervous or anxious energy in me. Basically, hot days make me feel like I'm back on a shitty mission in Iraq. As the heat and humidity increase, so do the uncomfortable sensations that my subconscious starts to bombard me with.

Now, let's assume it's a hot day, and I have to drive through the desert to get to work as I did when I lived in Las Vegas. My subconscious doesn't know the difference between the desert in Nevada and the desert in Iraq. All it knows is it looks and feels the same, and when it ties the desert together with heat, it ratchets up my discomfort level by making me anxious. Toss in a red car, similar to the one that smashed us out in Iraq, and my trip to work, thanks to my subconscious, could quickly turn from an easy drive into a roller coaster of panic, overwhelm, and losing my shit at the world.

When instances like this happen, even though I know they're not real, it doesn't do anything to change the fact that I literally have the sensation of worry, depression, anxiety, panic, or a combination of them all bombarding me from my well-meaning subconscious.

The understanding and coping skills I've developed do not come easy. On the contrary, I've spent years working on them, and I've come to realize that my subconscious, as a result of my PTS, goes off all the time. Constantly. My subconscious will ping me nonstop by sending alert sensations through my body. The pings feel like electrical energy, and as I said, they can be extremely uncomfortable. I get anxious from them, and early in my healing, I was getting pinged all the time.

When I was new to my post-traumatic stress recovery and working with my subconscious, it was difficult to understand

and deal with the body sensations. Something alerted my subconscious, and I was immediately bombarded with the sensation of agitation or something similar. So all day long, my subconscious was saying, "Hey, you're in a crowded area, *PING!*" because it didn't like the crowds in Iraq, Pakistan, and elsewhere. In those days, I had to always be on alert because I was in places with a high level of risk. Whether it was crowds or something else that caused an overstimulation of my senses, there would be some sort of perception-based stimulus, and "*PING!*"—I'm alerted whether it's warranted or not.

And, while my reactions today are a night and day difference from when I was in my PTS prime, when I find myself stuck in traffic, my subconscious goes crazy. Are those parked cars, out-of-control drivers, or roadside bombs? It doesn't know the difference. It just registers the trauma and alerts me. My subconscious doesn't understand that I'm stuck in traffic in the United States. I don't have to worry much about my car blowing up or a roadside bomb. My subconscious is trying to get my attention because it's worried about something from the past and trying to protect me here in the present.

Our difficulty is that, as humans, we mostly believe that our conscious minds run the show 100 percent of the time. Thinking your conscious mind doesn't run the show is uncomfortable and feels uncertain. Therefore, because most of you have the perspective that you are consciously running the show, you may largely discount, ignore, and refuse to explore why your subconscious is ringing the bell, sending up flares, and trying to get your attention. As a result, you completely write off the one part of your mind that is on 24/7/365, and if you explore and learn to understand it, it can provide a huge benefit to your life.

Now, while it's not always comfortable, I look at my subconscious mind showing up and goosing me with full anticipation and expectation. When it happens, and I'm in right alignment with myself, I can check in with my inner parts that are freaking out and reassure the part of me that's losing its shit that "it's nothing serious and we're okay."

When I do that with conviction and meaning, it often, but not always, dials down how it's pinging me. I intentionally use the term dial because the intensity of the energy that pings me advances and recedes as if controlled by a dimmer switch or app.

Why is that important? It's important because when I check in with my body and what my subconscious is alerting me to is real and not a false alarm, I'm ready that much sooner to avoid harm and capitalize on the opportunity.

Observational Capability

As discussed, the likelihood of detecting something in your personal environment is based on your observational capability. And, because you know what makes up success, you know that whether you're capable of detecting stimuli in your personal environment is dependent upon mindset, ability, and luck.

The OODA Loop–based Mind4Survival Decision-Making Process shows that the first part of your ability to observe is—yep, you guessed it—*mindset*. Are you aware enough to detect a change of state that occurs within your expanding horizon of lived experience? As discussed previously, if you don't notice a change, your baseline remains the same, and you will tend to operate as though nothing has happened.

Think of a person walking with their head down, totally focused on their phone, texting away with a friend. They may not notice a change in their situational baseline state, such as an ankle-breaking hole in their path or someone walking toward them with a knife in their hand. In the end, if you're not aware of a problem, you can't do much to avoid it.

When it comes to quantifying our awareness mindset, I base our level of awareness on Cooper's Colors, a color-coding system used to illustrate how our awareness, mindset, and observational capability work.

The brainchild of USMC Lieutenant Colonel Jeff Cooper (retired), Cooper's Colors is a tool for capturing the state of your mind in relation to your readiness to handle a situation.[19] What's important to understand with Cooper's Colors is not necessarily the colors but that your life consists of varying degrees of alertness, how those degrees interrelate, and how you relate to them when instinctively or intentionally increasing or decreasing your alertness.

White is when you are unprepared and unready to take action. You are oblivious to what's happening around you and consumed in your thoughts. You're not paying attention.

---

[19] John Dean Cooper, "Jeff Cooper's Commentaries," Jeff Cooper's Commentaries: Vol. 13, No. 1, January 2005, https://www.molonlabe.net/Commentaries/jeff13_1.html.

Next is condition yellow, which represents a state of alert but relaxed. It's kind of like what you are doing right now while reading this book, but you're aware enough to detect a stimulus in your personal environment.

Then there's orange, which means something has stimulated you. You are aware and alert; most of your focus is on the stimulus that triggered you. Orange means you are alert to a specific danger(s) and consciously/unconsciously preparing to take your alertness and actions to the next level.

Red is the condition you're in when you're ready to take drastic action. This is the stage when, after watching the oncoming car swerve toward her and her baby, a young mother positions herself in the best possible way to protect her baby and take the impact of the fast-approaching car.

Last, black is a widely used addition to Jeff Cooper's Color Code, although Cooper did not support it.[20] Black is the condition that accounts for the overload of your central nervous system during a freeze, flight, or fight experience. This is when your central nervous system hijacks and overpowers your rational mind and can take you down pathways that may not be effective for surviving, minimizing unwanted struggle, and living your best life.

This is why monitoring for alerts based on your external, classic-senses-based stimuli is important. It's also important to be in tune with your internal stimuli and sixth-sense body

---

[20] John Dean Cooper, "Jeff Cooper's Commentaries," Jeff Cooper's Commentaries: Vol. 4, No. 2, January 18, 1996, https://www.molonlabe.net/Commentaries/jeff4_2.html.

sensations. Do you have the ability to recognize, acknowledge, and understand those internal signals, give them credence, and set your awareness level accordingly?

Finally, your observational capability also requires a bit of luck. Maybe a sound you would not have heard otherwise bounces and travels. Perhaps you detect a new, yet faint, sensation pinging you—in that sense, luck may have been there to help you detect the stimulus.

What that leads to within the Observe phase of the Decision-Making Process is the last component of perceived reality—is a change of state detected? To reiterate, anything that changes your situational homeostasis, any stimulus in your personal environment, is considered a change of state. If you don't detect the change of state, you are unlikely to take effective action in response to the new stimuli.

Orient

Once you've gathered your perceivable data in the Observe phase, you are ready for the Orient phase. During the Orient portion of your situational awareness, you run your observed data through your filter of human nature and lived experience. This is where you pile all of your positive life lessons, along with all of the bullshit biases you allow yourself to maintain, on top of a mountain of beautiful, absolute, objective reality. The Orient phase is where you create perspective.

This is where you learn and sometimes force yourself to see things differently from others and differently from yourself from one minute to the next as you evolve. For example, you and I could both be looking at the same person standing in a driveway, but where I may see a trespasser, you may see a new neighbor you want to meet. Once we filter that information, we then use it to create new opinions and decisions. And, with decisions being a string of opinions one believes to be true, your decisions are nothing more than opinions, i.e., perspectives you believe to be true.

In Chapter 2, I noted that Endsley defines situational awareness as "the perception of the elements within a volume of time and space, the comprehension of their meaning, and the projection of their status in the near future." Using Boyd's Destruction and Creation theory and some of Endsley's concepts, let's unpack the definition a bit more to drive home its understanding and importance.

First, when defining situational awareness, Endsley states, "the perception of elements within a volume of time and space." I believe that situational awareness is how you perceive what is happening in the world around you and what is happening in your personal environment. Your personal environment includes all the elements you can detect through your external senses and subconscious alerts.

Your personal environment also includes everything that you *do not* or *cannot* detect, things you are unaware of. For example, you may be distracted in a crowd and not notice your long-lost friend two feet away. Again, you may not be aware, but that doesn't mean it's not happening.

The second part of Endsley's definition, "the comprehension of their meaning," starts connecting the dots of what you have detected. This is where you put meaning to, figure out, and understand what you observed, how that relates to you, how it relates to everything else around it, and how you relate to it right now. This is where you interpret and form conscious relationships with the current state of the elements in the present moment. This is the here and now.

Next, Endsley's definition mentions "the projection of their status in the near future." Now that you are aware of the elements within your personal environment, how they relate to you, and how they relate to one another, you can begin forming a perspective/prediction about the future of those relationships. You can use your perception of those elements to project a likely possible outcome or new baseline based on your understanding and belief about your observed data.

Decide

These next two portions of the OODA Loop, Decide and Act, are not components of situational awareness. That said, just like it's important to understand how mindset influences situational awareness, it is also important to understand how situational awareness influences your decision-making process and resulting actions.

The Decide phase is when you take the information you filtered during the Orient phase and use that to create a decision, opinion, or plan—something to move forward with.

Central Nervous System

Any time you make a decision, especially under the stress of a perceived threat, you experience the possibility of the central nervous system, in part or total, hijacking your decision-making process.

If you are relatively calm and balanced during your decision-making process, you will probably be pretty good at making an effective decision. Maybe, rather than explode on someone, you decide you need more information. Hence, you decide to return to the Observe phase, gather information, and refine your perspective on the situation. That may include considering the perspective of other people who you may typically disagree with, discount, or completely dismiss.

Your problems often happen when your central nervous system gets involved. It gives you the parasympathetic response option—freeze—and the two sympathetic nervous system response options—flight or fight. When your central nervous system is triggered, it is triggered by your perception of the data you inject into your decision-making from the Orient phase.

This is where my brain associates protecting a diplomat on a loud and crowded Iraqi street with a rock concert in the States. This is where your mind correctly or incorrectly perceives a threat and, as such, begins injecting the instinctual responses of the central nervous system. And it's when you start injecting central nervous system responses—and not necessarily good emotional responses—into your decision-making process that you often experience the worst impact on how you make decisions.

The central nervous system response level directly impacts the soundness of your decision-making. For example, if you slam a door behind me or sneak up on me, I will stiffen up and about shit my pants. It's my PTS-sensitive subconscious triggering a reaction from my central nervous system. It's my emotional response to loud noises causing me to bypass a rational response and, instead, go straight to a CNS freeze, flight, fight, or possibly crap myself response.

That doesn't mean that *any* emotional response is bad. In fact, sometimes it doesn't affect your decision at all. Maybe it prompts you to make a decision a little bit faster than you normally would have. A key, though, is recognizing when you're having a less-than-effective emotional response, figuring out the problem, and adjusting to have a more effective, positive response.

I feel the first milestone of effective decision-making is, after having already observed and oriented yourself to your personal environment, to *NOT* enter your decision-making riding a wave of ineffective central nervous system response. The more emotion and central nervous system response, the more opportunity you have to make a less-effective decision.

Looking at the Mind4Survival Decision-Making Process, you'll see that I have arranged four decision-making steps to help you have a fallback should your decision-making process become tripped up and a struggle.

My four-step process, which starts back in Orient, is as follows:

1. **Analyze the information.** This involves your perception. *Does this information align with my core values? Where did I get this information? Can I trust the source?*
2. **Identify the problem … or not.** Now that I know what the information is, is that a problem that needs to be solved or an opportunity I should consider?

3. **Develop options.** *Does this require a decision from me? Can it wait a while?* Be honest, critical, and kind to yourself. Generate several possible options or alternatives using a P.A.C.E. Plan—Primary, Alternate, Contingency, and Emergency plans.

4. **Choose your best option.** Once you have a clear understanding of the issue and it is time to move forward with one option, choose it and go. You can do a SWOT analysis—strengths, weaknesses, opportunities, and threats—by asking, *What are my capabilities? What are the advantages of going with that? What are the resources I need?* and so on.

Act

Action is what it says. You have four general outcomes:

- **Central nervous system.** An emotional freeze, fight, or flight response that, in part or total, bypasses the balanced decision-making process.
- **Intentional action.** You have walked through your decision-making process and have decided on an active, get-up-and-do-something action.
- **Gather more information.** You have determined you need to process more information before determining your follow-on actions.
- **Review past information.** You examine what you've done and experienced in the past or what others have done to establish a pattern of what worked and what didn't. You analyze this to decide upon an effective course of action.

A point to note about gathering more information and reviewing past actions. Both of these actions are often thought of as not taking action. However, appearing to take no action by letting the situation develop and instead gathering more information or further analyzing potential decisions is also considered an action response because you decided not to overtly act but rather pause and not rush blindly across an alleyway.

It's the decisions we make, not the actions we take.

CHAPTER 6

SURVIVAL

"**H**is hand! He's got something in his hand!"

My best friend was trying his hardest to warn me about the guy I was about to fight. It was one of those stupid fights you get into when you're an eighteen-year-old drunken idiot in a way-too-tight, fire-engine red tank top, trying to look cool while you're pounding wine coolers. It doesn't work.

So, I was the guy chosen to fight the aspiring gang banger; my options were to fight him myself or have the eight-ish of us fight the twenty-ish of them. "What's in your hand?" I asked him. Probably not the smartest move, but he was just as stupid—he showed me.

Unfortunately, I was too drunk to realize that it wasn't a roll of quarters until he sunk the knife into my side for the third or fourth time. And I only figured that out because he twisted it around a bit before pulling it out. Fortunately for me, seeing my blood on the outside of my body was more sobering than a Sunday morning IV in a Las Vegas hotel room.

The fear of dying hit me like a bolt of lightning, which gave me the briefest and most life-saving, central nervous system blast of out-of-my-head fight response: a one-and-done punch. He was down.

That bought us time to make a long dash to the car, with LA gang bangers on our tails throwing bottles and rocks. One of them caught up with us and launched a street sign through my buddy's mom's car windshield. My friends managed to get me to the hospital, where I eventually dealt with the fallout from a pissed-off Mom and Dad.

At eighteen, I was not doing my chances of survival any favors. I wasn't making good decisions. It was a wake-up call—I realized that it was only dumb luck that stood between life and death for me that night. I could not rely on luck to be there whenever I did something stupid.

In this chapter, we will look at how to stop relying on luck so that you can survive at even your lowest points. Survival is at the base of Maslow's Hierarchy and tells you exactly what you need to achieve to *survive*—not necessarily *live well*. "Living well" comes in the two fundamentals after survival: safety and self. Survival deals with just that—avoiding massive trauma and maintaining effective homeostasis, or as close to 100 percent effective homeostasis as possible. These are the most basic minimums that you need to survive.

The Survival Pyramid

To understand your survival needs and properly address them logically and effectively, the Survival Pyramid prioritizes your physiological survival requirements in order of precedence and need.

The Survival Pyramid expands on the Rule of Threes[21] to include important survival gaps based on my experience and Mind-4Survival philosophy. It includes both your homeostatic and non-homeostatic needs and, therefore, highlights both your physiological survival requirements (air, shelter, water, sleep, and food) and your non-physiological survival requirements (mindset, situational awareness, safety and security, and society). As such, the Survival Pyramid is the graphic representation of the priorities for human survival based on the speed at which unfulfilled requirements will result in your struggle and demise.

Not only does the Survival Pyramid focus on your physiological and homeostatic needs, it also includes some needs that Maslow didn't mention, which are also required for survival. Whereas the Survival Rule of Threes provides a roadmap of milestones that you must pass to move forward with life, the Survival Pyramid brings further order and detail to your needs-focused preparedness plans. With this tool, you'll know what must take priority, how to order your actions, and how to inform your decisions.

---

[21] The Survival Rule of Three is a set of guidelines that state how long a person can survive without the basic needs of air, shelter, food, and water in emergency situations.

Now, let's break down how that works within the Survival Pyramid.

Survival Needs: An Overview

After Mindset and Situational Awareness, my philosophy distills living down to three key areas: Survival, Safety, and Self. We've learned the tools and schools of thought that factor into this philosophy, so the remaining chapters will demonstrate how they apply to each of these areas.

Survival is the counter to death, and we will look closely at its fundamentals. Everything you do in your preparedness pays off—you prepare, not only to survive but to live your best possible life, right? Survival is the big hurdle—because after all, if you don't survive, it's game over for everything that follows.

When something shitty happens, that fraction of a second is the first chance you have to do anything. Within that short period of time, you collect the awareness to initiate any action, even if it is only to acknowledge to yourself, *All right, I'm in a shitty situation.*

From there, your awareness response will often include some level of central nervous system engagement: freeze, fight, or flight. Your preparations (known as "preps" in the prepper community) take the form of the things you can do ahead of time to mitigate or recover from threats to your safety and survival. These consist of how well you have prepared your mind and the physical skills, items, and systems you have in place to address whatever threat you are facing. The immediacy of availability could make all the difference.

There is a definitive progression of survival needs and an order of precedence. By breaking your survival needs into their most fundamental elements, you can zero in on exactly what needs to be addressed in order of criticality.

In total, built on a bedrock of mindset, the Survival Pyramid consists of seven levels (milestones) of basic human survival needs that escalate from the most time-sensitive survival needs at the base to the least time-sensitive survival needs at the top of the pyramid.

The pyramid's levels of time-based needs are as follows:

- Situational Awareness: one-third of a second
- Safety and Security: three seconds
- Oxygen: three minutes
- Environment: three hours
- Hydration and Sleep: three days
- Nutrition: three weeks
- Society: three months

As discussed in the last chapter, after your mental approach, survival begins with your awareness of an ongoing and developing situation.

From there, you move up the pyramid to safety and security, which is your ability to avoid a threat or take effective action in the moment to mitigate a threat.

Advancing up the pyramid from there is the next most immediate survival need: brain oxygenation. Knowing that lack of oxygen to the brain can cause unconsciousness and irreversible brain damage in three minutes or less, your first order of oxygenation business will be to ensure oxygen-carrying blood continues to perfuse your brain.

Next is your need to protect yourself from the harmful effects of extreme environmental conditions, including the impact of insects, wild animals, weather, landslides, and so on.

After that follows the need for water and sleep, so it's important to understand what happens in three days if you don't have access to either.

Nutrition is the next hurdle, so understanding your daily caloric needs is important to include in your preparedness plan. You can actually predict, with extreme accuracy, your ability to maintain effective levels of energy through food and nutrition.

Finally, your chances of survival increase greatly when you satisfy your need for society; essentially, this is the need for social interaction and support, someone to rely on when you are not at your best and, perhaps, closer to your worst.

Every elemental building block of survival is required to meet your survival needs, and everything you do to meet your survival needs has critical needs, too. You have a finite amount of resources—namely, time and money—so part of your greater understanding will be to prioritize how you examine your survival needs.

This chapter provides a system and framework for addressing your survival needs in a manner that allows you to make the best *informed* decision possible—it may not be the best decision in hindsight, but you work with the information at hand and go from there, hopefully giving it your best along the way.

Since it all starts with awareness, that's where we'll start, too.

Situational Awareness—One-Third of a Second

Your awareness capabilities are crucial, as they are key to avoiding or minimizing the harmful impacts of a threat or potential problem. Awareness may be the difference between living and dying. As discussed, your ability to make effective, situationally aware decisions determines whether your actions will be beneficial to yourself and others.

At one-third of a second, from the time a person becomes aware of a potentially life-ending event, unless they are well trained or experienced, the best they can usually hope for is to achieve awareness of the situation and acceptance. In other words, now that you're aware of the shitstorm you're in, do you accept that it's truly happening? This is where normalcy bias, confirmation bias, and the other factors of the human condition can come into play.

During this awareness phase, those most capable have the best chance of mounting an effective response for avoiding and minimizing a threat within a third of a second. I have found that when I'm overwhelmed, things get better if I take a split second to focus on something right in front of me, exhale a fast, deep breath, and confidently remind myself that *I've got this.* This method works for me, so long as I say it with intentionality and mean it. This usually helps me realign in the moment and get back in the game.

In terms of Cooper's Colors, it is not possible to live a life based in the red or even the orange. Instead of being on high alert all the time, you need to be able to ratchet it up and down when it's needed or when you believe it's needed. History and reality indicate:

- there will be times when you will not have effective awareness.
- there will be times when you need to unwind and relax.
- there will be times when shit just happens.

Most of us accept that life-and-death survival situations can happen out of the blue—but it doesn't make them any easier to accept in the moment when they're happening, especially when they are happening *to us*. It's unavoidable. When bad things happen out of the blue, outside your awareness, that is the worst possible place to find yourself.

I recommend a self-check-in when you figure out that you are stuck in the middle of a shitstorm. Check in to see if what you're doing or plan to do is as effective as you think it can be. Exhale deeply and ask yourself:

- *Is what I'm doing effective and helping the situation?*
- *Does my decision have some freeze, flight, or fight mixed in?*
- *If so, do I have too much central nervous system response mixed into my decision-making process?*

You may not be completely out of control, running around in a 100-percent central nervous system response. However, as long as you're not 100 percent there, you're good to go because you can begin working to use your rational thought to minimize the impact of your parasympathetic and sympathetic responses. As the impact of your central nervous system is normal, part of your preparedness is to learn to lessen the impact of your nervous system when it's causing some degree of ineffective response.

At its core, your preparedness relies entirely on preparations and luck. Hopefully, when you need it, your OODA Loop will evolve faster than the situation; my best estimate, from awareness to the potential for impact of an immediate threat, is about one-third of a second. That's the amount of time that, if you see a problem happening right now, you have to craft a response—oftentimes, responses you already have in your mind, ready to go. They are *almost* reflexive, but hopefully, you have absorbed as much information as possible in that split second of awareness to develop an effective action.

Safety and Security–Three Seconds

The next level of survival preparedness involves the capability to keep yourself and your loved ones safe and secure. Safety and security reflect your capability to safely avoid or respond to a threat that you don't avoid. Safety (threat avoidance) includes things such as getting out of the path of an approaching hurricane, not going to bad places at bad times, and not taking unnecessary risks.

Security includes your efforts to deal with potentially harmful situations that you don't avoid. Security responses include de-escalating verbal encounters, leaping into action to help another, and neutralizing threats when all else fails. And, as you can safely assume, the key to keeping you and your loved ones safe is an effective response to a threat or potential threat.

When you fail to safely avoid a threat, you must do your best to keep yourself secure by dealing with the threat as effectively as possible. In many worst cases, that means dealing with an immediate threat. An immediate threat is one that is happening right here and now. You must take immediate action to avoid the out-of-control car, to respond to the robber who just kicked your door in, or to stop the creep who is trying to walk off with your kid.

The key to successfully surviving the safety and security phase is the ability for fast and effective action to counter any potential harm. While well-trained people can respond to a threat within a second, most average people will take longer. Therefore, it's reasonable to assume the average person, should they not avoid a problem, will take about three seconds to respond to a threat.

This figure is based in part on a study by a police sergeant named Dennis Tueller. He surveyed a number of police trainees, asking them, "At what distance does an adversary enter your danger zone and become a lethal threat to you?" Tueller's study determined that his cadets could cover the traditional seven-yard distance in about one and one-half seconds.[22] Therefore, it would be safe to say that an armed attacker at seven yards is well within your danger zone. If a healthy male police cadet can cover twenty-one feet in one-and-a-half seconds, it is also reasonable to assume that many weekend warriors, while slower, can cover twenty-one feet in three seconds.

That's not to say we shouldn't shoot for being capable of a one-and-one-half-second, or better, response time. However, for most people with busy lives and limited training time, setting

---

[22] Dennis Tueller, How Close Is Too Close?, March 1983, https://uapdi.com/my/docs/tueller.pdf.

a more obtainable starting goal of three seconds not only helps build an effective immediate response, it helps build confidence too. The fact is, *in any situation that you are unable to avoid, you must be more effective in your response to a threat than the threat is effective in impacting your health and well-being.* If you don't actively deal with the problem by avoiding or outdoing it, you are left to the whim of the problem.

The goal of this level of preparedness is to avoid or deal with and effectively manage any threats that occur: an irate shopper gets in your face, the Christmas tree catches fire while you're eating dinner, a mentally unstable stranger pulls a knife, and so on. Ultimately, those who respond the quickest and most accurately have the best opportunities for success and survival.

Taking effective action increases your chances of survival and possibly someone else's. Maybe you're attending a friend's pool party and notice a child sinking to the bottom of the pool or see a look of distress on the child's face just before they sink. Hopefully, you already know that drowning doesn't always look like drowning (the way it's depicted on television or in the movies, with a bunch of thrashing and yelling for help) and that you must leap into action immediately with no forewarning whatsoever. The reality is that if you can't avoid a problem, then you may have no more than three seconds to understand there is a life-ending problem happening, and you have to take decisive action:

- What should you do?
- What is your plan?
- What are your preps?

When it comes to your safety and security, your actions and mindset should focus on what you can effectively do to mitigate the problem within three seconds of your entry into the situation. Therefore, when it comes to mindset, gear, planning, and preparation, everything you can effectively do to manage a three-second or less timeframe happens within this level of need—including the acceptance of the totality of your circumstances if that did not happen during situational awareness.

Not taking effective action to mitigate a threat is, as it sounds, not helpful for your survival. Work to rein in out-of-control responses that increase your vulnerability as soon as possible. Your awareness and action in response to a potential or emerging threat at this level will often result in you being entirely engaged in actively monitoring and dealing with the situation. Any mindset, gear, and preps that you use in this phase must be able to be put to effective use within three seconds. These types of immediate action items are the things you carry on you, have access to, and are ready to use within three seconds. So if you have something locked away in a backpack, trunk of a car, or out of reach, it's not a piece of immediate action gear. Instead, it's a delayed-action item.

This three-second phase reveals the importance of Boyd's OODA Loop decision-making process: when life and death are on the line, the side with the faster, more accurate decision-making process stands the best chance of winning. This is when your hard work, training, and dedication to enhancing your capability pays off. All of that repetition of thinking about options of various preparedness scenarios is training, and training sets you up to take faster, more accurate, and more effective actions to ensure your survival.

Have you mentally and physically rehearsed what you would do if your home were invaded? What about a strategy to tastefully place furniture near the front door in case it needs to be shoved in front of it to trip up potential home invaders? How about a family plan to leap into a strong defensive posture? As soon as the home invaders smash through your front door, what do you do? Have you thought about it?

Don't just talk about it—think it through. Imagine the sounds of yelling and screaming—how you will respond in such a high-pressure situation, where you must keep your head and wits about you. Imagine the fear, the anxiety, and the sheer shock of it all. What do those thoughts feel like? The deeper you feel it in your core, the better prepared you will be to respond to it. When the threat unveils itself, it's go-time—you have no more than three seconds to run, hide, fight, assess, respond, and take effective action.

You can use this approach to mentally prepare for all types of scenarios, such as an early morning house fire, natural disasters, a nearby industrial accident, etc.

Oxygen to the Brain–Three Minutes

After you have satisfied your survival needs for awareness, safety, and security, it's time to move to the physiological need for the brain to remain effectively oxygenated.

Once the oxygen flow to your brain slows down or becomes impeded, you are on the survival clock. The closer that clock gets to the three-minute mark and beyond, the more likely you or the person you're trying to help begin suffering irreversible brain damage. Therefore, once you survive any immediate threats to your safety and security, you can focus on making sure your brain and everyone around you are getting enough oxygen.

In terms of preparedness, I strongly encourage everyone to receive emergency bleeding control and CPR training. Then, review, practice, review, and practice the skills before you actually need them. This feeds your capability and allows you to act much sooner. Whether you watch videos or take an in-person certification class, you are improving your awareness to ensure everyone's brains stay healthy and operational.

Don't forget that while gaining awareness and expertise to increase your capability is incredible, it doesn't overrule your preparedness in terms of eating healthier, exercising the best you can, and being as mentally and physically active as possible. We all have our limitations. If you do your best to be as prepared as possible based on your reality, that is the best you can do, which is amazing!

When it comes to training, learning both how to control massive bleeding and how to help a person's heart and lungs circulate oxygen to their brain provides, in my opinion, the most enduring life-saving capabilities that the average person can know. And that, if used, can greatly impact themselves and others—potentially including loved ones. The bottom line is that *everyone*, when capable, should learn CPR and bleeding control.

The progression from maintaining a healthy homeostasis in the form of effective oxygen to the brain and death is as follows:

- Between 30 and 180 seconds of oxygen deprivation, loss of consciousness is possible.
- Three minutes: brain cells begin dying.
- Five minutes: neurons suffer more extensive damage, and lasting brain damage becomes more likely.
- Ten minutes: death is imminent, even if the brain remains alive. Coma and permanent brain damage are almost inevitable.
- Fifteen minutes: survival becomes nearly impossible.[23]

In short, as soon as a person's melon starts becoming oxygen-deprived, they start to slide from the here and now toward it's-been-nice-knowing-you unconsciousness. Unconscious people cannot take action.

Whereas CPR adds oxygen to a person's bloodstream and helps to circulate it to the brain, hopefully buying the person in trouble priceless seconds and minutes, bleeding control attempts to stop the blood from leaving the body so quickly—taking the life-sustaining oxygen with it and possibly killing the person in under three minutes.

Massive uncontrolled bleeding can quickly result in hemorrhagic shock. A healthy adult can lose about 20 percent of

---

[23] Spinalcord.com Team, "What You Need to Know about Brain Oxygen Deprivation," SpinalCord.com, April 26, 2021, https://www.spinalcord.com/blog/what-happens-after-a-lack-of-oxygen-to-the-brain.

their total blood volume before feeling complications such as weakness, lightheadedness, shortness of breath, and low blood pressure. A person can easily lose three or more pints of blood in just a couple of minutes and enough to be beyond saving in as little as three minutes.

When it comes to emergency bleeding control, where seconds count, a person must also be able to effectively apply a tourniquet to save an injured person's life. (That also means they must already have a tourniquet ready to go.)

At most, you have three minutes to go from zero to hero. Do you have the awareness, understanding, and equipment to step in and save yourself or someone else? Do you have the capability to keep the oxygen flowing when everything goes south? If not, you can learn to do it—it just takes some effort on your part.

Environmental Protection–Three Hours

Once you've ensured your oxygenation needs are met, you have bought yourself a little time. In addition to addressing any new threats popping up out of nowhere, you can now focus on protecting yourself beyond the capability of your immediate-action response and expand toward the protection of—and protection from—the larger space around you.

Outside of dropping a giant rock on your head, the environment can harm or kill you in a number of other ways:

- **Exposure to extreme conditions such as extreme heat and extreme cold.** In addition to protecting yourself with what you are wearing—your immediate-action

gear—you have to be able to protect yourself for the long term.
- **Other living things**, regardless of whether it is a predatory animal, insect bite, or plant.

I remember well my platoon sergeant shivering so badly during a frigid training mission in Louisiana that he looked like he was having convulsions while standing up. All of the Rangers in my unit lost weight due to shivering our asses off to retain body heat and avoid hypothermia.

Hypothermia happens when a human body's core temperature drops below 95°F (35°C). It can onset in as little as five to ten minutes of unprotected exposure to the cold, with the following symptoms:

- Shivers
- Blue hue to the skin
- Altered level of consciousness
- Difficulty speaking
- Memory problems
- Altered judgment
- Loss of coordination
- Apathy[24]

If not reversed, none of those symptoms are conducive to long-term survival. Therefore, the second you notice any of the signs

---

[24] "Hypothermia," Mayo Clinic, April 16, 2024, https://www.mayoclinic.org/diseases-conditions/hypothermia/symptoms-causes/syc-20352682.

of hypothermia, the survival clock is ticking. Getting warm is critical. You have to reverse the cooling process, whether that means wrapping up in a blanket, climbing into a sleeping bag, lighting a fire, turning on the heat, getting off the cold ground, or snuggling up with someone warm. Otherwise, the body will continue to lose its ability to maintain homeostasis and slip off into the forever-after by freezing to death.

On the opposite end of the climate spectrum is surviving extreme heat. After spending years living in the Middle East, Africa, and other places that are almost melt-your-face hot, I cannot describe that level of heat to those who have never experienced it. It's like living in a convection oven that threatens to cook any exposed skin. Just as hypothermia follows a specific path when moving from healthy to dead, survival problems from heat exposure follow a similar, albeit hotter, path.

The first level of heat injury is heat cramps, which are quite painful, short-lived cramps often involving the calves, thighs, and shoulders. When struggling with heat cramps, a person's muscles may jerk involuntarily and spasm.

The second level of heat injury is called heat exhaustion, which happens when a person's core body temperature rises to between 101°F (38.3°C) and 104°F (40°C).[25] Heat exhaustion is a type of heat illness that can be caused by exposure to high temperatures and overexertion.

---

[25] "Exercise-Related Heat Exhaustion," Johns Hopkins Medicine, March 4, 2024, https://www.hopkinsmedicine.org/health/conditions-and-diseases/exerciserelated-heat-exhaustion.

Signs and symptoms of heat exhaustion may include the following:

- Nausea
- Headache
- Dizziness
- Heavy sweating
- Cool, moist skin
- Fatigue
- Faintness
- Rapid pulse
- Muscle cramps

Left untreated, heat exhaustion can lead to heat stroke, and heat stroke leads to death. As the next level of extreme heat injury, heat stroke occurs when the body's core temperature is over 104°F (40°C). Symptoms include the following:

- Absence of sweating
- Dry skin
- Confusion
- Disorientation
- Agitation
- Coma
- Death[26]

---

[26] Cleveland Clinic medical professional, "Heatstroke: What Is It, Symptoms, Causes, Treatment & Recovery," Cleveland Clinic, September 13, 2021, https://my.clevelandclinic.org/health/diseases/21812-heatstroke.

The likelihood of a heat illness increases with strenuous activity and rising humidity levels, so it's important for anyone who is active in the sun or spends time outdoors during the summer months to recognize symptoms and be prepared to take action immediately.

If the heat illness is caught and effectively treated in time, the person should fully recover. The first step is to cool them. If the person is doing anything strenuous, have them stop and loosen their clothes. When possible, move them to a cooler location and start cooling them down by fanning them. If you have water, drench them with it. If the person has the mental awareness to drink fluids without choking, have them slowly drink some cooling fluids—ideally, liquids with electrolyte replacements, but water will still work.

When it comes to surviving the heat, the best way to survive, besides staying out of it as much as possible, is to stay hydrated.

Hydration and Sleep–Three Days

You burn off water through natural body processes and interaction with the environment, so it stands to reason that your water must be replenished. When it comes to hydration, a person without water can perish within three days, usually when it's hot outside. Even if you're not dead within three days, you will be impaired.

The process of perishing from dehydration includes the complications from heat illness that occur during exposure to the environment. Symptoms of dehydration also include the following:

- Decreased skin elasticity
- Dizziness
- Nausea
- Seizures due to electrolyte imbalances
- Kidney failure
- Death[27]

Remaining hydrated is fairly simple: drink plenty of water. The general rule for water consumption is 15.5 cups per day for an adult male and 11.5 cups per day for an adult female. On a weekly basis, the average adult will, at a minimum, need 7 gallons of clean drinking water, and a child will need 2.5 to 3.5 gallons per week, depending on their age.[28]

Staying hydrated is simply based on your age, activity level, and environment. With water consumption or any preparedness-related health question, please confer with your health provider to get professional advice specific to your needs. Once you feel thirsty, you are already behind on hydration, so stay ahead of the hydration game by being deliberate about your water consumption.

---

[27] "Dehydration," Mount Sinai Health System, accessed August 11, 2024, https://www.mountsinai.org/health-library/diseases-conditions/dehydration.

[28] Mayo Clinic Staff, "How Much Water Do You Need to Stay Healthy?," Mayo Clinic, October 12, 2022, https://www.mayoclinic.org/healthy-lifestyle/nutrition-and-healthy-eating/in-depth/water/art-20044256.

Just as you can't go more than three days without water, you also cannot go more than three days without sleep—or rather, you *shouldn't*. Sleep deprivation can lead to mental impairment, hallucinations, and questionable survival decisions.

The negative impact of sleep deprivation escalates with time. Twenty-four hours without sleep can result in a mental impairment equivalent to having a 0.10 alcohol level. So basically, you are as effective as a functional drunk trying to survive, and your body begins to shut down.

After two days without sleep, your body will begin to force "microsleeps" for several seconds to half minutes, usually followed by periods of disorientation. Microsleeps happen regardless of what you are doing. These are forced sleeps that your body makes you have once you have passed a certain threshold of sleep deprivation. So, when you are in the process of making your most important survival decision and haven't slept in two days, a microsleep may shut you down and put you to sleep right in the inconvenient middle of your survival efforts.

Once a person has 72 hours of sleep deprivation, they can experience extreme concentration, perception, and other mental problems. At three days without sleep, you may see things and people who aren't there; trust me, I have been there, and at that point, you're not in the most effective control of your survival anymore. And when you are not in control of your survival, you are not prepared to survive.

Nutrition–Three Weeks

The simple, nonscientific fact is that your body needs energy to operate. Your body requires nourishment, typically food, to provide it with the energy it needs to operate. Without food, the human body begins to eat itself to continue operating. The longer you go without eating, the more likely you are to experience symptoms associated with lack of nutrition:

- Weakness
- Dizziness
- Low blood pressure
- Low heart rate
- Dehydration
- Heart conditions
- Organ failure
- Neurological conditions

A person may die after 21 days without food, but even if they live a bit longer, they are completely ineffective in handling anything that has to do with their survival. By then, their body will be revolting, so they will have little to no effectiveness in acting on their own behalf.

Nutrition has a pretty simple formula: energy in, energy out. That formula is directly influenced by how many calories you consume to fuel the machine, and you are the machine. If you put less energy into your body than you use, you lose weight and eventually die.

Therefore, the goal of surviving is as simple as maintaining a surplus balance of consumed energy versus expended energy. A general rule of thumb is to plan on 2,000 calories per day for adults. However, some recommend 2,600 calories per day for an adult male. So, to play it safe, research calorie requirements that are specific to your situation. Consult with your doctor, nutritionist, or another expert on your and your family's age and situation-based nutritional needs. And yes, people with special dietary needs can prepare to meet those needs. Gluten-free, high protein, keto-tastic, or whatever floats your healthy preparedness heart. So don't listen to the nay-sayers who say you can't be a prepper with special needs. That's why it's called preparedness.

Society–Three Months

In his 1651 book *Leviathan*, English philosopher Thomas Hobbes (1588–1679) wrote:

"Whatsoever therefore is consequent to a time of war, where every man is enemy to every man, the same consequent to the time wherein men live without other security than what their own strength and their own invention shall furnish them withal. In such condition there is no place for industry, because the fruit thereof is uncertain, and consequently no culture of the earth, no navigation nor use of the commodities that may be imported by sea, no commodious building, no instruments of moving and removing such things as require much force, no knowledge of the face of the earth, no account of time, no arts, no letters, no society, and, which is worst of all, continual fear and danger of violent death, and the life of man, solitary, poor, nasty, brutish, and short."[29]

In many ways, Hobbes was pointing to the need for society. The benefits that come with society—public safety, healthcare, water, power, and sewage—are often overlooked when people prepare. Typically, preparedness stops with stocking the cupboards and addressing individual and family needs.

In my opinion, this is a major flaw in most preparedness paradigms. Part of what enhances your preparedness is the expansion of it beyond your individual capability; one person cannot know and do everything. We need to build a society, even if we begin that building with just one other person.

So, why three months? Just as the need for water and food is not a hard-and-fast three-day or three-week rule, the need for society doesn't have a hard-and-fast rule either. The three-month marker simply serves as a reminder that, at some point, we all need support and interaction with others.

On December 3, 2019, my girlfriend at the time wrote the following Facebook post: "These two kitties need a loving home ASAP. They are both about fifteen years old and have lived together as a pair since they were kittens. They are completely house-trained and compatible with other animals. Ms. Kitty, the black cat, is extremely loving and sensitive. She loves to cuddle and can always sense when her humans need love. Mr. Cat, the Siamese, is super intelligent, loves sunshine, and enjoys

---

[29] "Early Enlightenment Thinking," Thomas Hobbes, accessed August 11, 2024, https://www.webpages.uidaho.edu/engl_258/lecture%20notes/thomas_hobbes.htm.

interacting and playing with other animals and humans. Please share!!! Feel free to message me for more info." She closed the post with a big heart.

The cats were mine. I wasn't able to feed them, and she was unable to take them. I was five months out of my six-week post-traumatic stress recovery trip to Utah. I was safe from suicide but couldn't hold it together to keep a job. Walking my golden retriever, my ride-or-die buddy, a couple of times a day was more akin to climbing Mount Everest than a simple dog walk.

I had been out of work long enough that I had blown through all my savings, maxed out every credit card I could get, and pretty much wrecked my finances. I hit my fifties, and my father was paying my rent. And even with that assistance, I was still broke. I couldn't afford to feed my cats, and my ability to feed my dog was dwindling on life support and circling the drain fast. That was the day I went to a level of hell that I didn't think possible.

Every decision I had made—good, bad, and indifferent—led me to this point. It was the last place I ever imagined myself—considering that only a couple of years before, I was clearing $170,000 a year, plus bonuses, as a misguided corporate executive with an MBA. Two years later, I couldn't afford to feed my cats.

That's the day I lay in the middle of the kitchen floor, curled in the fetal position. It was worse than the day I had signed myself into my post-traumatic stress recovery program. Even on that day and my last survivable option, I had the autonomy to lock myself away or free myself; I was still independent—it was my choice. December 3, 2019, was the day I realized that I had no other choice. The only choice I had left was the decision to ask for help—the kind of help a six-week stay in Utah couldn't provide.

That's the day I ran out of hope for a miracle to help me—when I knew and accepted that I couldn't do life on my own. I was out of options other than admitting I'd lost the battle and conceding the excitement of the ride had taken a toll on me—that is if I wanted to be around to battle some more in our war of life. It's all I had, and it was one of the most vulnerable things I could do, which makes it one of the most honest and freeing things I've ever done. At fifty years old, I had to admit that, while I tried as best as I could manage, I'd lost the battle.

I had to do the one thing that, as a trauma-induced, preparedness-minded person who is gearing up for the shit to hit the fan (SHTF), I feared most. I had to rely on others. What made it worse was that I had to be vulnerable enough to let the people who loved me the most help. That seemed insane to me at the time.

Despite all my preparedness, that was the day I knew I was done trying to isolate myself from the rest of the world—mentally, physically, and emotionally. We all think we can manage on our own just fine, but we are kidding ourselves. The fact is, we need others. We need help to do it right. And while I believe it takes time to develop a lasting and trusting relationship, we need to establish relationships in the here and now before disaster strikes.

Now, disaster and common struggle can definitely bring people together, and it's not a good plan to think you can handle a bad situation alone. The bottom line is that when it comes to survival, we need others. When we are sick, we need others. When we are injured, we need others. I might have a good mindset for safety and security, but I don't have a good mindset for fixing things, growing things, or tons of other things.

They say it takes a village to raise an idiot, and I'm here as living proof. In my case, my village was my nearly eighty-year-old dad who supported me, my best friends, my incredible therapist, and my sister and highly cat-allergic brother-in-law, who took my cats in so that I could, eventually, bring them back home with me. My village consisted of all the amazing people who, for years, had my back without me even realizing it.

To successfully build your village, you must be willing to be open, honest, empathetic, and engaging. Maybe your society starts with your significant other, your family, or others. You define your society, which operates within the larger society of communities, regions, cultures, nations, and so on.

When building your personal community, decide what kind of tribe you want to be a part of. Do you want to assemble a group of people, similar to a Dungeons and Dragons party, based on their skills and resources? Or do you want to create your version of society with people who are aligned with your core values—with whom you can develop personal, caring, trusting, and long-lasting relationships?

At the low points, even the worst of enemies can become allies, and life can be a series of the-chips-are-down, suckfest moments. When life is a series of good times interrupted by the occasional bad time, we are better served by developing loving, supportive relationships over superficial ones based upon expediency. The great thing about people who are values-aligned is that they typically enjoy spending time together.

All you need to do is look at the images of hurricane evacuation routes a day or two before a hurricane, with all the people fleeing. If you have a good personal network and community of like-minded friends, perhaps you'll have somewhere to go where you will be welcomed with open arms. Similarly, you can be available if people need to come to you in their hour of need. And if you have a community larger than yourself, you increase your options, capabilities, and the support your village can provide in your hour of need as you do in theirs. And that isn't something that should only happen when times are hard.

What if you are more prepared than others in your tribe? It's easy and normal to feel frustrated with those who don't prepare; after all, people who don't prepare will be up shit creek without a paddle when disaster happens. And while being up shit creek without a paddle may be true for the unprepared, it doesn't have to be—we have some control over that.

While preparedness is my thing in my tribe, it doesn't have to be theirs. Instead, I love to learn about their perspective and what makes them tick. They know I'm a prepper; I know they're not, and they're good at so many other things that I'm not. They make me a better, more capable person just by being in my life.

In turn, when they don't prepare, I do my best to prepare for them as much as possible. One thing we have to be careful about is overwhelming others about preparedness—people shouldn't ever be scared into preparing. You're not motivating others by handing them an oversized plate of intimidation smothered in doom, gloom, and fear.

In fact, scare tactics may send them in the opposite direction. Remember, when we have an emotional mindset, we are less likely to make effective decisions and more likely to revert to our cognitive biases.

Survival of Our Species

When it comes to the survival of our species, one of the greatest hurdles to not going extinct is for us to evolve to the point where we can survive the worst calamities possible. In the case of our current iteration of the human species, the worst possible calamity is the earth's destruction.

The universe is a dangerous place. Therefore, the reality of preparedness, as it relates to the human species, is that the human race must work together to find a reliable and sustainable way off our planet. After all, it is only a matter of time before the earth or our ability to survive on it is destroyed. We must figure out our capability, as a species, to survive—just ask the dinosaurs. Oh, that's right—we can't. They went extinct due to an unforeseen and unprepared-for cataclysm.

The ultimate survival goal is, for us as a species, to protect ourselves by preparing effective, sustainable, off-planet living opportunities. Again, this is about our survival as a species—a species that has all of its eggs in one basket. And that basket of eggs is hurtling through the universe, a universe we know very little about.

I don't pretend to be smart enough to know how we get off the planet and live the true off-grid, homesteading experience, only that it needs to happen as soon as possible. And the only way we do that is if we all figure out the biggest threat to the human species: the impact of our bias- and belief-filled versions of the human condition. It's our bullshit, which is also part of the human condition, that promotes cultural and regional tribalism and prevents us as a species from focusing on what is truly important—being the best species we can be. That starts with each of us being the best humans we can be, living the best lives we can lead. That's what society is all about. And that's what survival is all about.

CHAPTER 7

SAFETY: MANAGING RISK AND OPPORTUNITY

In 2010, I sat on the outskirts of Baghdad, reading an email from my roommate back in the States. He informed me that our house had been robbed while he was out of town for Memorial Day weekend. The culprit was a crackhead so skinny that he was able to break out the tiniest window of my home and slide through. He (and I suspect others) then ran through the house, tearing through our lives and violating the place where we were supposed to feel most safe. He knew he'd struck gold when he spotted a closet door with a deadbolt on it.

If there is a deadbolt lock on an interior door, there is often something inside worth locking up. And there was. My safe, full of valuables and irreplaceable family heirlooms, was inside. In addition to the irreplaceable items he took, what was also gone forever was my unrealistic hope that we could ever be completely secure in our homes.

At that point, I was a security professional with a bachelor's degree in security management. I knew how to manage risk, and I didn't do it. I was lazy and hadn't taken the time to protect my home the way I knew I needed to. Yes, I put a deadbolt lock on the closet door that held my safe, but I also knew the flimsy door needed to be replaced—and I didn't do it. They got everything and literally wheeled my safe out the front door, all because I just didn't get around to doing what I knew I should have done—manage my risk.

Managing Risk

Using the tools of mindset and situational awareness, *how* we prepare ourselves mentally directly affects how we prepare physically. Risk management lies between the two and determines how we manage our most important and personally valuable assets, the threats that can harm our assets, and the vulnerabilities we have in our preparedness to mitigate the threats. After we meet our survival needs, managing risk helps us answer the question, "Now what? Where do I start?"

Risk management is where you can make a deliberate effort to eliminate bias from your decision-making process by using an objective approach to meeting your ongoing safety, security, and preparedness needs. Risk management is where you build much of the confidence that comes with being on the right track and crushing life as best you can.

Once you have met your survival needs, the next step is to manage your risk and opportunity as effectively as possible. Unfortunately, many people in the preparedness world look at risk with the perspective that we're trying to minimize and stop everything negative. That's not what we are trying to do because we can't stop every negative thing from happening.

What you are really working toward is making the most of the *opportunity* to reduce the negative impact of a harmful event.

Preparedness is not negative. Rather, it is the opportunity to minimize the bad stuff that happens. When approached correctly and responsibly, preparedness is a positive, confidence-building, and freeing opportunity. Free from worry and a required dependency on others.

You get there by understanding and effectively managing your risk and opportunity.

In developing the content for the rest of this chapter, I relied heavily on insight gained from years of incredible conversations, support, and friendships with Ed Clark and Tristan Flannery. Ed is a retired Special Forces Lieutenant Colonel and CEO of Executive Interface, and Tristan is a former Army Ranger and globally recognized business strategy and risk mitigation expert. Both are exceptionally well-versed in the science of risk management and have a significant influence on this chapter.[30]

Risk and Opportunity

What is risk? For the purposes of risk management, Ed defines risk as "the likelihood of a harmful event." A harmful event occurs when a threat—a person with ill intent or a hazard such as a natural disaster or another unlucky event—negatively impacts something or someone we care about.

---

[30] You can learn more about Ed's work at executive-interface.com and Tristan's work at orbitalrisk.com.

Opportunity, on the other hand, is a positive risk. Taking a cue from Ed's definition of risk, opportunity is the likelihood of a beneficial event, which happens when something enters your environment that, if you can capitalize on it, may positively impact you and your life. Opportunities come in the form of a beautiful sunset, a new friendship, a better job, improved preparedness, happiness, etc. When it comes to opportunity, the risk is often the risk of missing an opportunity.

How you manage risk and opportunity is key to achieving a better life; the more effective your management, the better your life can be. While risk has a negative impact, managing it provides you with the opportunity to find the positive.

The bottom line is that preparedness is not only about managing and mitigating risk, it is also about capitalizing on opportunity.

Carpe diem!

Your Risk Profile

Now that you've made it through the survival phase, it's time to make your life safer and less worrisome.

To do that, you must understand how to objectively (with minimum bias and emotion) compare your constantly fluctuating risks and opportunities as equally as possible. You must be able to compare risks equally and objectively with one another to judge which risks are most likely to cause the greatest harm should they happen. Understanding which risks are the most problematic in relation to one another allows you to paint the overarching picture.

Your risk profile is an objective view of everything you have to protect, everything you're protecting it from, everything you're protecting it with, and the consequences should you lose what you're protecting. Therefore, understanding your profile provides you with the reality-based information you need to make the most effective decisions possible regarding how you manage your risk and, ultimately, your life. That's not to say you can't add emotion and bias to the process. I'm saying, though, that creating your risk profile provides you with information you know to be as accurate as possible. How you make use of that information is up to you.

Risk Register

I prefer to create my risk profile by comparing and contrasting risks using a risk register. A risk register is a hierarchical list of assets prioritized by individual risk scores based on the culmination of the three primary risk factors: threat, vulnerability, and impact. It's your primary risk factors that, when combined using the risk formula, produce an individual risk score for each asset. As such, the risk register and its primary risk factor data are the building blocks of your risk profile.

It's incredibly easy to create your risk register. Start by grabbing a piece of paper, dividing it into five columns, and labeling each column in the following order: Asset, Threat, Vulnerability, Impact, and Risk Score.

Risk Register				
Asset	**Threat**	**Vulnerability**	**Impact**	**Risk Score**

The risk register, through the primary risk factors of each asset, includes everything you need to determine the impact should an asset be lost or suffer damage due to a threat and your vulnerabilities.

When it comes to understanding the factors that make up your risk profile, I base the primary risk factors on Ed Clark's risk management philosophy by asking myself four simple questions:

1. What do I have to protect? (These are my individual assets.)
2. What do I have to protect it from? (These are the threats to my assets.)
3. What do I have to protect it with? (Once I know what I have to protect my assets, I also know where I'm lacking. These are my vulnerabilities.)
4. What's the impact (consequence) if my asset suffers harm? (What harm do I, my family, and my situation suffer now and in the future.)

Assets

When determining your risk profile, the first question you should ask yourself is, *What do I have to protect?* This question is best answered by writing down everyone and everything you feel you have to protect. If that feels difficult and overwhelming, you're right; it can be. Once you get started, though, you'll catch a rhythm and understanding, and over time, you'll get to exactly where you need to be with capturing your assets and adding them to your risk register.

While it can be overwhelming to put this amount of conscious effort into the vulnerabilities and threats that you haven't considered or, at least not to this extent, you do have a hack to help make it easier. The hack to covering all of your assets is based on the fact that, according to Ed, "every life system, no matter how simple or sophisticated, can be broken down into four basic types of assets":

- Life: family members, friends, and loved ones—both human and animal
- Nonconsumable Assets: home, vehicle, electronics, clothing, and so on
- Consumable Assets: food, fresh water, air, cash, medications, gasoline
- Intellectual Property: reputation, personally identifiable information (passport, birth certificate, social media data), computer files, and inventions

When considering what you value, I like to think about areas of my life based on how I live and the assets associated with each of those areas. I encourage you to keep it real and simple, like work, play, and home. You'll likely find all four types of assets within each area, making it easier to create a more thorough list for your risk register.

For example, what needs protection at your workplace? People? Files? Cash? At home, maybe it's your family, pets, cell phone, and a safe full of valuables. In terms of play, maybe it's the bowling alley, gym, and other places where you let off steam or have fun. In the end, approaching your assets by area is an excellent way to construct a comprehensive risk profile.

Now, getting back to your risk register, create a number of rows under the headings row equal to the number of assets you plan to add to your risk register. Then, enter one name, title, or another identifier into each row of the "Asset" column. For this example, I'll enter Family Member, Bike, Truck, Food, and Flash Drive (memory stick) of photos down the left-hand side of my risk register in the cells underneath "Asset."

Risk Register				
Asset	**Threat**	**Vulnerability**	**Impact**	**Risk Score**
Family Member				
Bike				
Truck				
Food				
Flash Drive				

Threat

With your assets identified and added to your risk register, it's time to ask yourself, *What do I have to protect my assets from?* The answer to that question is your specific threats and hazards, which are the things and events that, if and when they happen, can result in harm or loss to your assets.

Threats include motivated and capable living, breathing, planning, and harmful people, animals, insects, bacteria, viruses, and other yet-to-be-confirmed life forms. Next, hazards are based on the frequency and intensity of events, such as storms, fires, earthquakes, other natural disasters, and random occurrences of harm-causing luck that happen whenever Mother Nature and Fortune are ready to educate us about the reality of our existence.

An asset's threat score is determined by its likelihood and capability. Likelihood, in the case of a living threat, is measured by the threat's motivation to harm the asset. Similarly, hazards of nature and chance are measured by the frequency of the hazard over time—how often does a severe storm hit or a bridge collapse versus a supervolcano eruption or an asteroid impact?

When it comes to the basic risk formula, threats and their likelihood and capability are likewise measured on a scale from 1 to 5:

1. Low Threat: Low likelihood or capability to cause harm.
2. Minor Threat: Some likelihood or capability to cause harm.
3. Moderate Threat: Moderate likelihood or capability to cause harm.
4. High Threat: High likelihood or capability to cause harm.
5. Severe Threat: Severe likelihood or capability to cause harm.

With the threats to your assets identified, your job is to work your way through your risk register, assigning threat scores of 1 to 5 based on the motivation (frequency) and capability (intensity) of your threats and hazards.

An example of how individual threat scores are calculated can be illustrated by comparing the threat of having my bicycle or truck (nonconsumable assets) stolen from my driveway. In the case of my bicycle, it's a hunk of junk that all but the most desperate of criminals will avoid, making its threat score a 1. My truck, on the other hand, is relatively new and shiny, and with a vehicle theft ring occasionally operating in the area, I rank the threat toward my truck as a 3. With the risk to my transportation options figured out, I'll then complete my risk register, where my research has determined that the likelihood of a threat harming a family member, my food, or digital photos all rank as 1.

Risk Register				
Asset	Threat	Vulnerability	Impact	Risk Score
Family Member	1			
Bike	1			
Truck	3			
Food	1			
Flash Drive	1			

The more you do this, and the more you refine your scoring, the better you will be at knowing, understanding, and prioritizing the greatest threats to you and your family in as much of an objective, reality-focused manner as possible. And that's what risk management is all about.

Vulnerability

The next primary risk factor to consider is vulnerability. Vulnerability is your lack of preparedness. Unlike preparedness, which measures your capability to mitigate and recover from harm, vulnerability is your inability to prepare for, defend against, and recover from it. Vulnerability can also be thought of as a general weakness or weakness to a specific threat(s).

As with impact and threat, your vulnerabilities are also measured on a range from 1 to 5:

1. Low Vulnerability: Well prepared, minimal risk.
2. Minor Vulnerability: Mostly prepared, some risk.
3. Moderate Vulnerability: Moderately prepared, moderate risk.
4. High Vulnerability: Partially prepared, significant risk.
5. Severe Vulnerability: Unprepared, severe risk.

With that, I'll continue completing my risk register. Let's assume that I keep the bike and truck in the driveway, up near my home, and that there are a few motion lights in the yard and driveway. The bike isn't locked and is leaning against the house within easy view of the street—in other words, my few, if any, theft prevention efforts (lack of preparedness) equate to a high theft vulnerability. While the theft vulnerability is high, the fact that I have no need or intent to replace the bike if it is stolen makes my ability to recover from the loss high. When considered in combination, my lack of mitigation efforts and easy recoverability from the loss of the bike give me a vulnerability score of 3.

My truck, on the other hand, is always locked, has an alarm system, and is pretty difficult to steal, making my theft mitigation efforts fairly strong. Similarly, my comprehensive insurance that covers theft makes my ability to recover from the harm of a threat fairly significant as well. Therefore, I rate the overall vulnerability of my truck as low, a 1.

Using that same thought process, I then work through the rest of my risk register, rating my family members, food, and a flash drive of digital photos as 1's because they're safe and secure in my home.

Risk Register				
Asset	Threat	Vulnerability	Impact	Risk Score
Family Member	1	1		
Bike	1	3		
Truck	3	1		
Food	1	1		
Flash Drive	1	1		

Impact

The impact of losing something important to you is a measurement of the consequence of losing that asset. The consequence of losing your asset is based on the duration of loss plus a combination of the personal, financial, or other values placed on that asset. For purposes of the basic risk register, the impact of losing an asset is based on the below 1 to 5 scale:

1. Low Impact: No noticeable effect on daily life.
2. Minor Impact: Minor inconvenience, easily manageable.
3. Moderate Impact: Significant disruption, manageable with effort.
4. High Impact: Major disruption, significant financial loss or stress.
5. Severe Impact: Critical consequences, extreme personal or financial loss.

For my example risk register, I will grade the loss of a family member as having a consequence of 5. On that topic, while most lives are precious, not all hold equal value to everyone equally, and in the end, the loss of any asset is specific to your risk register and is relative based upon the impact on you and your risk profile. For example, compared to losing a close family member, losing a neighbor whose name I barely remember isn't as impactful, so the guy next door gets a loss impact score of 1.

Again, this is based on how the loss affects you. For example, in my case, while I loved my goofy golden retriever and BFF (best furry friend) Koah, his loss, while personally devastating, did not equate to the loss of a close family member but definitely rated higher than the neighbor I don't know next door. Each one of you may feel differently because, in the end, this is your risk register, so make it your own. The key to the risk register is that the three primary risk factors—threat, vulnerability, and impact—are treated in an objective, apples-to-apples comparison so that the output—the risk score—provides you with a true, objective hierarchical picture of your risk profile.

Continuing with my risk register, I may rate the loss of my old bike, which hasn't been ridden in five years, as a 1. The tires are flat, the chain is rusty, and it's an eyesore, but it's my eyesore, and as such, its loss has a low impact on me.

I'll rate the loss of my fully insured truck as a 3. Yes, while dealing with the insurance company and figuring out my driving options for the next couple of weeks would be disruptive to my life, I'd have a replacement vehicle as soon as my insurance kicked in. While I'll rate the loss of my truck as a moderate impact, another person with no insurance or only liability coverage and little to no savings may rate the loss of their vehicle as a high impact—a 4 on their risk register. Perhaps they will be unable to work if they lose their car. Maybe you're fortunate enough to have a second vehicle, so losing one vehicle would have only a minor impact score of 1.

Next on the register, the impact of the loss of food (a consumable asset) depends on each person's specific situation. For example, whereas a person who is broke or near broke might grade the loss of their food as moderate, a person with a stack of money may not think twice about the loss of food. That, however, could change as each person's circumstances change. Should both people be caught in a disaster where acquiring food becomes difficult and uncertain, both could apply an updated grade of 5 (Severe Impact) to their risk register, raising their overall risk score to reflect the evolving situation.

Finally, let's focus on the intellectual property of an external flash drive full of digital photos. And, yes, one can argue that the flash drive is a hard asset. However, in this case, I feel that the years of photos and videos on the flash drive are more consequential than the flash drive itself, so I'll include the flash drive as intellectual property. Unfortunately for the digital photos, I only rate their loss as a minor inconvenience with a score of 1.

With that, applying the asset loss impact score, my risk register now looks like this:

Risk Register				
Asset	Threat	Vulnerability	Impact	Risk Score
Family Member	1	1	5	
Bike	1	3	1	
Truck	3	1	3	
Food	1	1	3	
Flash Drive	1	1	1	

The Basic Risk Formula

With my primary risk factor data complete, it's time to follow the basic risk formula and calculate the score for each asset on the register. Basic risk scores are calculated using the following formula:

$$\text{Threat} \times \text{Vulnerability} \times \text{Impact} = \text{Risk Score}$$

Computing your basic risk score requires simple multiplication. Multiplying your asset's threat score by its vulnerability score, followed by its impact score, all on a 1 to 5 scale, provides a helpful separation of risk scores when the risk register is complete. I recommend starting with the values as presented to get a feel for it. You can expand the range, however, I believe it's very easy to overcomplicate the process. Try to stick to this basic 1 to 5 scale as much as possible in the beginning.

The final output of the basic risk formula is each asset's risk score, which ranges between 1 and 125. With that, the only significance you need to give to the resulting numbers is their position in relation to one another in establishing the hierarchy of your risk profile. Other than that, the final numbers are simply a tool to help you understand how to better manage your risk. In short, don't get wrapped up by the final number—it's all relative.

As a result of using the methodology discussed here and after sorting by risk score, my risk register and the picture it paints (my current risk profile) grade my truck as having a risk score of 9, my family member a 5, my bike a 3, food a 3, and the flash drive of photos a 1.

Risk Register				
Asset	Threat	Vulnerability	Impact	Risk Score
Truck	3	1	3	9
Family Member	1	1	5	5
Bike	1	3	1	3
Food	1	1	3	3
Flash Drive	1	1	1	1

Understanding Your Risk Profile

Now that your risk register is set, it's time to read and understand the risk profile picture it paints. In this case, let's start with the obvious—the risk score for my truck is higher than the risk score of my family member. Does that mean I have to rush into a burning garage to save my truck over saving my family member? No, it means that the risk of harm to my truck is greater than the risk to my family member. Therefore, based on my objective data, it makes more sense, risk-wise, to dedicate my time and resources to protect my truck. That is, until my risk profile changes.

Ultimately, risk management allows you to understand the true, objective-based ebb and flow of your risk, which allows you to more effectively manage your risk profile. In one of our recent conversations, Tristan Flannery summarized it to me this way:

> When I think about risk, I always view it as what is likely to happen. And what is the impact? The same holds true with opportunity. The reality is that there are risks and opportunities everywhere. There is always going to be risk and opportunity.
>
> There's a risk that I'm going to get in a car accident while driving down the street. Likewise, there is the opportunity to avoid a car accident while driving down the street. But in consideration of both, what are the likelihood and probability? And what is the impact in the end?

The impact of risk and opportunity is situationally dependent. For example, the impact of risk to me is going to be much more significant if I'm driving on the freeway at eighty-five miles per hour than if I'm driving through a school zone at fifteen miles per hour. And with that, the risk of hitting a child with my car is much greater when driving through a school zone at fifteen miles per hour than on a freeway at eighty-five miles per hour.

In the end, managing your risk profile depends on your mindset and ability to understand the fluid and developing nature of your personal environment in the moment and project that understanding over time. If that sounds familiar, it is. It's very similar to Endsley's definition of situational awareness that I discussed earlier. And what is your risk profile? Nothing more than in-depth and ongoing, objective situational awareness about your changing risk.

Monitoring Your Risk Profile

To understand your risk profile, you must first understand your risk factors and how they relate to one another.

At this point, some may ask, "How do you know when you should reevaluate your risk factors?"

You can find the answer in the definition of risk management: "the continuous process of evaluating and addressing risk." Risk management is something each of us should do on an ongoing basis.

Managing risk doesn't mean being paranoid. Instead, it means having situational awareness that is in balance with your needs so that you can detect baseline shifts in threats and vulnerabilities, which equate to a baseline shift in risk.

As life changes over time, so does risk. And, similar to life, risk changes both in the moment and at specific milestones in time.

Sometimes, risk changes in the moment:

- When you enter or exit a freeway
- A loud bang on your front door
- Walking to your car at night
- Meeting a stranger for the first time
- Learning that bike and car thefts are on the rise

Sometimes, risk changes over time:

- A newborn suffocating in its crib
- A toddler sticking something into a light socket
- A young teen being abducted
- An older teen driving while intoxicated
- A middle-aged person experiencing job loss and financial hardship
- An older adult suffering a slip-and-fall injury

You can reevaluate your risk factors by simply paying attention—again, practicing situational awareness—to your constantly evolving personal environment. When any of the three risk factors change, it's time to reevaluate.

Ed likes to use the term *spurious risk management* to describe an almost reactive management approach when problems are overlooked or ignored and not addressed until something big happens—*big* being relative to the individual and the situation. If you are not consistently monitoring your environmental baseline for shifts in your risk profile, you are not as situationally aware as you can be and, as a result, will be more prone to spurious risk management and overlooking problems.

Hopefully, what you're learning here will help you avoid falling prey to that. If you are situationally aware, you are more deliberate about reengaging with your risk factors to determine if something feels out of whack concerning your risk profile.

For example, let's say you return home to discover that your front door is open. You never leave it open, so what is the likelihood of a threat inside your home? Perhaps it was the wind. Perhaps it wasn't. What do you do? Do you enter your home? Do you go to a neighbor's house? Do you call the cops?

If you unexpectedly find a door open, you should automatically assume that your risk profile has increased. You have a higher risk because an unknown event has occurred. Yes, it may be the wind—or it may be something much worse.

What do you have to protect? If you're single or your family isn't home, then the asset you have to protect is you. Some people may consider protecting their stuff more important than their life; however, most of the time, stuff is just that—stuff that's not worth losing your life over.

What do you have to protect it from? You don't know why your door is open. In this case, you have to protect yourself from the worst possible options that may have opened your door. Is there a burglar, a home invader, a stalker, or a rapist who followed you home from the store waiting inside?

What do you have to protect it with? Are you a tactical genius, or do you have extraordinary superpowers? Even if you are and do, are you prepared to overcome the criminal's luck factor? You can protect yourself by not going into your home, opting instead to go to a neighbor, ask for help, and call 911.

What's the impact if my assets suffer harm? What happens if you decide to enter and a bad person is inside, waiting to do bad things? Do you end up in the hospital or worse? What about the impact on your family and friends? What's the consequence to your future well-being, confidence, anxiety, and worry?

By not going into the house, you—likely the most important thing to protect—have protected yourself. By not going inside, you've removed the likelihood of the threat causing harm to you by mitigating almost all possibilities of encountering the threat. Your decision not to enter the house is all you need to protect yourself. Action does not always mean confrontation. Protective action can—and whenever possible, *should*—begin with avoiding confrontation—including the *likelihood* of confrontation. Once you have asked yourself the four risk-profile-determining questions, your risk profile should be higher because the door is open, and what is beyond the breach is unknown.

If your risk profile isn't higher after discovering an unexplained open door, you should step back and consider whether you are suffering from some sort of cognitive bias that minimizes the potential seriousness of the situation. If your door is open and you don't know why—your risk has definitely increased!

Then, you make your decision:

- Do you mitigate the risk by not going into your home?
- Do you accept the risk and head into your home?

Until you go inside or somebody comes running out, you have mitigated and minimized your risk. The minute you go in, you have accepted the risk. You're saying, "I don't know what's in there, and I'm willing to go in there and accept the consequences *anyway*." Your action will then determine the impact you will face from the risk. If nobody is inside, your impact is low (you may have an elevated heart rate and some anxiety), or you may confront a familiar or unfamiliar person with unknown intent.

Personal Accountability

It's imperative to understand that successful risk management requires personal accountability. This is how you avoid going down the dangerous path of spurious risk management.

Personal accountability demands that you proactively work to stay aware of and then address any detected changes in your risk profile by reevaluating your risk factors. In addition, you want to avoid emotionally charged reactions. Proactively managing risk will help alleviate that.

Instead of reacting to an emotionally charged assumption about your risk, examine your risk profile questions to find out exactly what changed, why it changed, and how you can best address it. Then, force yourself to systematically observe and analyze your risk through your risk register. This will help you take ownership of the situation, how your actions can improve it, and how it might devolve beyond your control.

When taking ownership, you should be conscious and deliberate about how you look at your life and respond to changes in your risk profile. Beyond an open front door, maybe you get a weird vibe about a stranger. This should immediately alter your risk profile. What about a notification from your security camera? Again, it changes your risk profile. Do you notice the vehicles around you when you're driving so that you are aware if you're being followed? And do you have a plan in place if you are? (Hint: it may be best to drive straight to the police or fire department.) These are not uncommon occurrences and should set off the risk profile alarms in your head.

Your Mind4Survival includes the decisions you make on a daily basis that not only focus on your survival but also on your safety, comfort, and what you do to live your best possible life. For example, you can take every cent you have and spend it right now; you have the freedom to do that, but is that a good idea? Probably not. It's probably a very bad idea that should send your risk profile into high alert.

When it comes to managing your risk profile, it's essential to understand that every decision you make impacts your probability of success, whether its impact is positive or negative. You should view your risk profile through the same lens of every decision: assess its impact, positive or negative, and analyze the risk versus the opportunity.

This also eliminates the burden of trying to plan and prepare for the zombie apocalypse because your risk profile should ascertain that "The Walking Dead" coming to life is highly improbable. When we calculate the risk of a zombie apocalypse using our risk register, the risk, if we're honest, will be 1. Therefore, instead of preparing for a zombie apocalypse with no realistic probability of happening, you can prepare for more-likely-to-affect-your-life scenarios.

Maybe on an icy morning, for example, you're the victim of a random slip and fall—one of the most significant contributors to death in the US. Being laid up in a hospital or even at home reduces your ability to generate income and provide for your household.

Your slip and fall caused you and your family to come up short of the goals of preparedness because you are suffering unwanted struggle. And had you not spent every last penny preparing for the zombie apocalypse, you may have had money available for a fancy new snow shovel and pet-friendly deicer, which would have reduced your risk of slipping and falling on the ice.

In another scenario, perhaps your Mind4Survival has you examine your risk of future job loss and your career potential. You decide that advanced education in a trade, business, or something similar will expand your potential to earn a larger and more stable income. You then receive whatever education or training is required to help stave off any future problems with income and the ability to maximize opportunity.

The bottom line of risk management is that to effectively manage risk, you start with these four questions:

- What do I have to protect?
- What do I have to protect it from?
- What do I have to protect it with?
- What's the consequence if I fail to protect it?

Now that you've looked thoroughly at the elements of safety and risk, let's zoom out. Remember that we started with survival because it addresses our need to survive in the moment (Survival). Once your in-the-moment survival needs are met, you can focus on expanding the options to meet your long-term survival needs (Safety). After ensuring you have the ability to meet your needs consistently and over the long term, you then have the opportunity to work on yourself so that you can live your best possible life (Self).

CHAPTER 8

SELF: EIGHT TRUTHS TO LIVE YOUR BEST LIFE POSSIBLE

Teddy Roosevelt captured the essence of self so well in his famous speech, "Citizenship in a Republic":

> It is not the critic who counts; not the man who points out how the strong man stumbles, or where the doer of deeds could have done them better. The credit belongs to the man who is actually in the arena, whose face is marred by dust and sweat and blood; who strives valiantly; who errs, who comes short again and again, because there is no effort without error and shortcoming; but who does actually strive to do the deeds; who knows great enthusiasms, the great devotions; who spends himself in a worthy cause; who at the best knows in the end the triumph of high achievement, and who at the worst, if he fails, at least fails while daring greatly, so that his

place shall never be with those cold and timid souls who neither know victory nor defeat.[31]

The Mind4Survival philosophy focuses on preparedness for mindset, situational awareness, survival, safety, and self. In the last couple of chapters, we outlined the goals of survival and safety:

- The goal of survival is … well, to *survive*.
- The goal of safety is to live a safe and secure life.

In this chapter, we'll address the goal of self, which is to be the best *you* possible to live your best life possible.

What Is Self?

This may sound a bit nuts (welcome to my world), but I found it really difficult to come to grips with my understanding of *self* as it applies to my Mind4Survival. With regard to the fundamentals of preparedness, if you are satisfying needs that neither ensure survival nor make you any safer, do they actually matter? If the world turns to crap, all of that is out the window, right? No, that's not right.

So what is self?

Self provides you with a roadmap for dealing with your instinctive requirements of life. It provides you with the most

---

[31] "The Man in the Arena: Citizenship in a Republic," Theodore Roosevelt Association, accessed August 28, 2024, https://theodoreroosevelt.org/content.aspx?page_id=22&club_id=991271&module_id=339364.

wonderful result of preparedness: the opportunity to live your best possible life.

The concept of *self* empowers you to recognize your needs and desires, granting you the capacity to make choices instead of being driven solely by emotional reactions to the human condition. Even though you have walked through eliminating emotion from your decision-making as much as possible, your desires *will* influence your thought process and behavior and ultimately help determine whether and how you go about not only surviving but truly living.

How you live your life is perhaps the most important aspect and outcome of your fundamentals of preparedness. Do you live a life that is safe, loving, rewarding, and fulfilling, or do you lead a life that is not true to yourself?

Self is the fundamental that makes all your effort with mindset, situational awareness, survival, and safety really worthwhile. It is more than basic instinct; self is the fundamental that gives us a higher reason to prepare and a reason to live when doing so may be incredibly difficult. Going back to Maslow's Hierarchy, self is why we have the need to self-actualize.

For skeptics who believe this has no business being mixed in as a fundamental of preparedness, your motivation as humans is based upon your needs. And it's your needs that influence how you approach and interact with the world around you.

Therefore, while you can survive and lead a happy life without self-actualization, and many of us do, your need to self-actualize and grow beyond yourself does influence your interactions with everything within your personal environment. So if *self* represents the top of Maslow's Hierarchy, what can you do to fulfill your self-based needs, knowing there are no guarantees?

The best way to fulfill your higher-level needs is by minimizing risk, overcoming struggle, and being in the right relationship with some of life's basic truths—how you approach them and improve your potential to optimize them. I have come up with eight basic truths that I use in my life that help me along the way, and I'm taking the rest of this chapter to share them with you. All of these are loosely based on the Serenity Prayer.

(Note: These may sound like a crunchy mix of the metaphysical, motivational, and moronic. Fair enough. Take them in, and stay open to what might speak to you. Read for insight rather than agreement. Modify them to fit your own path.)

Truth #1: Know, Love, and Live Your Core Values

Core values are your fundamental beliefs, which guide your actions, decisions, and priorities throughout life. Ultimately, the differences between a good and a bad decision are your values and how you feel (your perspective) about the decision you are making.

While you already know that even when you try to make a decision based 100 percent on facts, the determination to make that fact-based decision is based in emotion, with the choice itself being at the root of your decision-making. Your core values help you stay focused on what matters most and form your thought processes accordingly.

Perspective will twist facts and lead to different conclusions for different people. As the current climate of our nation's discourse shows, the world is full of differing perspectives and viewpoints. As you know, none of us sees reality for what it is—the impact of the human condition prevents us from seeing reality as anything other than our individual perspective. Therefore, you should do your best to make sure the emotion at the foundation of your emotional decision-making is based on the things that you hold most dear—your core values.

When I am successfully acting and making decisions aligning with my core values, I feel more at ease and settled. When I feel more settled, I find that I'm also happier, more fulfilled, and more in the zone of living my best life possible. That's not only a goal of preparedness—it's the goal of life.

Take some time to think about what's important to you—what you believe in, what sort of person you want to be. Once you have a good understanding of your core values, you can start working on and living them every day.

Do what Amy Crawford, PhD, has everyone in her trauma recovery program do: start by brainstorming a list of values that are important to you.[32] Some examples could include family, friends, health, happiness, and freedom. Other examples of core values are bravery, creativity, determination, forgiveness, friendship, gratitude, honesty, humility, kindness, patience, perseverance, and self-control. Search around to find the values that are most important to you. Use the terms and values

---

[32] To learn more about Amy and her work as a trauma specialist, visit amyleecrawford.com.

discussed here or those that you find elsewhere to create your master list.

Once you have a list of your core values, think about what beliefs or principles are important to you about those values. For example, if family is important to you, some beliefs or principles could be loyalty, trust, and respect. If health is important to you, some values could be taking care of yourself, being healthy, and living a balanced life.

If you find that living by your core values makes you happy and fulfilled, those choices are probably good for you. If not, then it's worth exploring other beliefs or principles until you find some that do.

You can create your list by doing an internet search for "core values list." In my experience, the lists are hit-and-miss, but by looking at several, you can put together your own. Once you have an initial list in place, it's time to start eliminating those that aren't as aligned with your beliefs as the others are. As my perfectly tough therapist, Amy Crawford, had us do, start by eliminating half the values on the list. Then, when you're ready, eliminate half of the remaining values. Repeat this process, thinking and feeling your way through the values until, over time, you can whittle it down to a brief but power-packed list of three to four values that describe and define who you are and what you believe. This will help you live a life that is authentic and meaningful.

Make sure that your actions reflect your core values. For example, if one of your core values is family, then make and dedicate time for them. It's easy to get sidetracked, but if you want to live by your core values, you need to focus on them. When you're feeling tempted to do something that goes against your deepest convictions, take a step back and remind yourself why those values are important to you. If you're doing something and it doesn't feel right, take a moment to reflect on whether what you're doing aligns with your core principles.

When you find that your actions are no longer in line with your core values, it may be time to make a change—different choices or new priorities. For those of us who struggle with not feeling fully satisfied with our decisions or lives, this can be from a difference in our aspirational values (values we hope to be true and aren't) and lived values (the values we actually live by). If this rings true for you, this may be a one-step-at-a-time process to allow your priorities and decisions to fully align with your aspirational values. It's okay to change over time as long as you do your best to remain true to your core values.

Truth #2: Embrace Your Struggle

German philosopher Friedrich Nietzsche wrote, "What does not kill me, makes me stronger." In other words, certain milestones that include struggle, discomfort, and difficulties mark our path to a greater understanding, fulfillment, and self-defined success.

Earlier in the book, I mentioned that the first noble truth in Buddhism is that life is a series of ongoing suffering and struggle. It's the nature of life itself to include struggles and challenges that ultimately can be leveraged for your self-improvement. Struggle can provide context to experience love, respect, and self-actualization more fully.

On the flip side, life without struggle is a life never truly understood, experienced, and possibly never truly successful. Without struggle, you can fall into complacency and take things for granted.

For example, I would not be writing this book had it not been for all my struggles. It was only through my unwanted war with post-traumatic stress that the current iteration of my philosophy and approach to life materialized. Without my many years' worth of mental and emotional suckfest—where my measurement of success was that I made it through another day without eating a gun—I would not be here to write this.

I don't recommend my path because many do not make it out, but I suggest that whatever struggles you are currently facing, step back and see them as refining experiences that will get you closer to who you really are and who you are supposed to be. Struggle can be purposeful as long as you view it as such.

Your forays into struggle, sacrifice, and suffering do not all hinge upon life's curveballs, either. Life presents you with two types of struggle: wanted and unwanted. Both offer opportunities for self-improvement as you minimize their negative impact.

Since wanted struggle finds you seeking out discomfort and difficulty, you have to want to suck. For example, almost everything we did in the Rangers sucked. And if it didn't suck, we'd usually find a way to make it suck. Rangers love the suck so much that they take an already epic session of struggle and misery and find a way to make it suck more, thus achieving a victory for having survived something that sucks to the degree it did.

Everyone in the U.S. Army is issued a field jacket—a great piece of equipment to keep you warm. Since the Rangers love to make something suck even more, you were never allowed to wear your field jackets. After all, if you're going to have the reputation of being hard, you might as well play the part harder, not smarter, right? That did not mean you were not responsible for maintaining two inspection-ready field jackets in your locker. As I said, if it could suck, the Rangers would make it suck more. And while turning up the volume on the suck wasn't appreciated by many of those new to the Rangers, it eventually grew on you. If it didn't, you got out.

Therefore, the level of sucking experienced by the Rangers is voluntary, making it a type of wanted struggle. Why should we eventually come to welcome the suck? It had more meaning because it was difficult, and succeeding at really difficult things is a core value of the Rangers.

Your wanted struggle may not include working in freezing temperatures without a field jacket or forced hydration sessions followed by push-ups that leave you vomiting. Maybe your wanted struggle is making sure you do some level of exercise three times a week or putting in a garden to save money on food. By increasing your amount of wanted struggle, you can increase your understanding of unwanted struggle, which allows you a clearer view of reality.

Wanted and unwanted struggle are two sides of the same coin. Wanted struggle sharpens your perspective and helps you develop a better understanding of unwanted struggle. This then fine-tunes your ability to make better decisions that result in taking the most effective actions possible, which provides you with the greatest opportunity to live your best life possible.

Truth #3: You Define Your Success

If you know me personally, you know that I drop f-bombs like most people pepper their eggs. The fact that I have made it to the last chapter of this book, keeping my mouth mostly in check, shows enormous restraint on my part, and now I'm going to blow all of that up.

Alas, one way that helps me live my best life is by saying, "Fuck success." Yes, that's right. *Fuck success.* I'm not saying to fuck *your* success; I'm talking about fuck your ideas of success that rely on the opinions and definitions of others.

Philosopher Albert Schweitzer stated that success is not the key to happiness—happiness is. If you love what you are doing, you will be successful. Therefore, success is based on whether you truly love what you do. Since love is an internal feeling, your success is also internal and comes from within you. So the question of whether you are successful is yours and yours alone to answer.

Sometimes, it takes our whole lives to learn that we can choose to define the parameters of our success, which is, oftentimes, a feeling that we are seeking. Ultimately, other people's opinions should not matter when it comes to our definition of success and whether we have achieved it.

Don't accept the externally prompted desire to measure up to the standards that some try to pin or project onto you. When you do that, you are basically taking other people's standards and trying to measure up to what their idea of success is for you. We betray ourselves and our future when we make it about what others think of who we should be and how we should live, work, play, and love. To break free of the boxes you've allowed yourself to be placed in, you need to be willing to define or redefine what it means to be successful in your own life. Then, make decisions that are based upon your internal values, standards, boundaries, and vision, paving a road toward living your best life possible.

Of course, there will be times when some decisions are not as good as others—it happens. When it does, we tend to beat ourselves up over it, but a better alternative would be to consider what you have learned from it and how you can make better choices next time.

There are also times when others will try and derail you by talking trash or blowing smoke up your ass with praise. During these times, remember your core values, embrace your struggle, and always do your best anyway. It makes it much easier to tell other people to piss off when you're doing right by yourself.

Ultimately, life is full of choices. The question is, whose drumbeat will you march to—your own or someone else's? It's never too late to start choosing. Life is one big beta test, and you are worth trying and trying again.

Truth #4: Understand and Acknowledge What You're Preparing For

When it comes to preparedness, it's important to understand the magnitude of what you are preparing for. If your level of preparedness has motivated you to learn CPR, for example, you are preparing to be the person who gets down on your knees and pumps on someone's chest to keep another's heart beating and their brain oxygenated. You are going to be their heart and lungs. You are signing up for that—and that is a powerful thing.

If you are into preparedness like I am, you are preparing for a long-term macro disaster, where you plan to be on your own for weeks or longer. In prepper terms, you are preparing for a shit-hits-the-fan (SHTF) event, something that causes society to go belly-up and our way of life to fall apart—neighbors fight over food, and suffering occurs on an unimaginable scale.

While it may seem odd, when I came to terms with what I was truly preparing for, it gave me hope and a sense of security. That's because I know I am better prepared to handle an unlikely large-scale event, which means I'm more capable of handling life's hiccups and smaller-scale events that are likely to happen.

Many times, we want to avoid the situation or what we fear may be a worst-case scenario. We don't like to think about starvation or unsanitary conditions. I would argue that understanding what you're preparing for exposes you to the struggle you could face; this helps you navigate your own OODA Loop quicker and more accurately and thus make more effective decisions. When it comes to life and death, that makes all the difference.

Then, there is the aftermath—preparing for the aftereffects of the traumatic experience. Some land in, and remain in, a form of mental struggle. Others process their memories and never seem to experience a bump in the road. Others, like myself and many of my friends, still find ourselves struggling more to survive after the fact than we did during the act of surviving.

Truth #5: Prepare for the Aftermath

To help illustrate what "prepare for the aftermath" means, I want to share some of my post-traumatic stress recovery with you, the foundation of which is largely based on the teachings and insight of the amazing team at Deer Hollow Recovery in Draper, Utah.

After being home from overseas for a couple of years, I started having problems. Panic attacks, agitation over small matters, chest pains—I felt like I was falling apart; I couldn't hold it together and had no idea what was going on. It all came crashing down on August 30, 2017.

At the time, I was a director for Triple Canopy, a large private military company (PMC), where I managed their contract with the United States Department of State Diplomatic Security Service. My program provided diplomatic security personnel to protect the U.S. diplomats serving in high-threat countries. I began my time with the State Department about a dozen years before when I served as a Personal Security Specialist-Paramedic with Blackwater, protecting U.S. diplomats in Iraq.

When I woke up that Wednesday morning, things were definitely worse than usual. It's hard to describe, but in a nutshell, I was a wreck. I felt like I had been awake for a week while somebody had worked me over with a baseball bat. My hands shook. I was agitated, confused, and couldn't catch my breath. I felt like I was dying.

After trying to rally and give it a go in the office, I couldn't do it anymore. Something was wrong with me, and I needed to get to the emergency room fast. One of my team members took me to the hospital, where they conducted the standard tests for someone who thinks they're dying. Fortunately, everything checked out fine except my blood pressure, which was through the roof and wouldn't come down. When I asked the doctor what she thought the problem could be, she responded with a sledgehammer of the obvious: she asked if I'd ever had my head examined.

Okay, maybe she didn't put it quite that way, but she did wonder if I'd ever worked with a professional who could help me deal with some of my life experiences. Until that moment, I didn't realize I had a big, whopping case of post-traumatic stress and that this was the sign that it was time to get serious about dealing with the aftermath of living through years of tragedies and personal cataclysms.

The question that most plagued my mind was, *How does post-traumatic stress work?*

I always reasoned that if I understood the problem, I would be better prepared to find a solution. At the time, I didn't believe PTS was really a thing and had spent years in denial.

Unfortunately, PTS is very real, and if you spent decades in war zones and elsewhere, experiencing the worst humanity has to offer, what is the likelihood that you might have it? On August 30th, I found out.

Once I understood that PTS is a system of shitty, unprocessed memories that can hold great power over you and your mind, I knew I needed to hack into my trauma by first understanding it and learning the mental tools to help me process it.

This meant getting into the anatomy involved. In the front of your brain, behind your forehead, resides the prefrontal cortex, responsible for rational thought. The prefrontal cortex also plays a role in engaging the parasympathetic nervous system, which is essential for controlling sympathetic nervous system responses of the amygdala at the base of the brain. That's where the limbic system, which is responsible for emotions and memory formation, resides.

The limbic system contains the amygdala, which is responsible for detecting fear and engaging the sympathetic nervous system. It's your sympathetic nervous system that is responsible for your fight-or-flight response. The parasympathetic nervous system is responsible for freeze and your regulated state. It is your built-in instinct that, as part of the survival mechanism of human nature, is designed to take control away from you during a survival emergency because having an extended mental debate over the proper course of action isn't always a great idea when your life is on the line.

The central nervous system is hardwired as part of the human condition, but it cannot distinguish between past traumas and current-day, real emergencies and problems. Whenever my post-traumatic stress gets ratcheted up, I try to remind myself that what I'm experiencing is a result of my internal desire to protect myself. That helps me separate facts from incorrect subconscious-generated sensations.

In my case, the PTS-associated agitations and emotions hit me as vibrating waves of energy, and the intensity of those waves elicits a corresponding emotion. The energy feels like a constant and uncomfortable, low-level shock that runs through parts of my body.

For example, the electricity that I feel when I'm depressed feels like a low-toned hum that emanates from the top of my abdomen. Meanwhile, my agitation has a higher-pitched, faster-vibrating sensation of not-so-good-feeling electricity flowing through my upper abdomen, chest, and center back. Anger has a more intense sense of electrocution that covers a larger area of my body, including my shoulders, the base of my neck, and so on. The more my PTS is activated, the more I feel these uncomfortable and sometimes painful electrical sensations flow through my body.

After spending a lot of time exploring the sensations that happen in me, I've learned that the sensations I physically feel happen before the emotional responses of depression, agitation, and so on. The physical sensations are warning signals initiated in my body by my subconscious mind to alert my conscious mind that, based on past experiences (trauma), it thinks there is some sort of threat looming. In other words, the terrible sensations I get due to my PTS are signals from my subconscious mind, trying to get my conscious mind to take action and, in so doing, help me achieve the goals of preparedness.

I say all this because it affects my understanding of what, specifically, I am preparing for. If I'm only paying attention to the signals from my subconscious and not using my conscious mind to work through what exactly is going on, my preparedness will be more knee-jerk and less thoughtful. We already know that, in terms of preparedness, reactive isn't as effective as proactive.

An emotional response is where the amygdala gets involved and triggers some nervous system response. In other words, you may have little to no input into how you respond to that situation. When I was at my worst, the thought of doing the most basic tasks, like taking a shower, seemed Herculean in scope. Overwhelm was my norm. I would spend most of my days trying to calm my mind by smoking a mountain of pot and watching Joe Rogan—all while overwhelmed by unprocessed memories of personally horrible shit, like not being able to get the blood out of a buddy's eyes before zipping up his body bag.

Unprocessed memories caught in my subconscious were wreaking havoc in the present. In my early PTS days, my only relief came from my therapist, Alana Jackson, PhD, who kept me together and from killing myself.

So what does that mean? It means that our minds don't always get it right. Therefore, when my subconscious pings, regardless of the intensity, I try to remember to check in with it and see if its opinion is warranted. If it is, I can put that into my OODA Loop and begin figuring out the situation. However, if my PTS has hijacked my mind, and what I'm feeling isn't based on current events and the situation in the present moment, I try to remind myself that I'm not in a shit storm and that everything is okay.

Understanding the physical signs and sensations that may be pinging you helps manage the situation when your central nervous system is activated. When it's triggered, you can do a self-check-in to see if your energy is guiding you correctly. If it isn't, try to regulate your nervous system to feel calmer and more rational using the techniques I discuss below.

We all struggle, and some struggle results in trauma. I think it's fair to state that we're living in a traumatized society, even though many would not consider themselves victims of it. And, because of the nature of life, if you aren't traumatized now, you stand a fair chance of becoming so after disaster strikes.

A quote attributed to the ancient philosopher Rumi says, "The cure for the pain is the pain." The hope is that, through hard work and processing, we can make the pain of our past trauma less powerful, less overwhelming, and less burdensome in the present. Understanding this about ourselves gives us greater insight into what we are preparing for and helps us modify what seems more trauma-induced than reality-induced.

Calming Techniques

Cope ahead for situations that might be stressful. For example, going to the DMV stresses me out. So I drive to the DMV a day or two before I have to go to make sure I know where I'm going and how to get there. I visualize the crowds and people sitting inside, waiting for their number to be called. I make sure I have any paperwork ready the day before, and when that day finally comes, I am better prepared and more confident to handle the situation, and it doesn't suck as much as it used to.

Reframing is a skill that can help change your perspective. Who doesn't want to scream at the bonehead who cuts you off in traffic? Reframing involves telling yourself that they didn't mean anything by what they did, that what they did may be the best they are capable of, and that you should chill out. Try making up a story about why the guy in the red car just cut you off. He's late for work, his kid got in trouble at school, his boss is a jerk, and his wife just reminded him that he forgot to pick up milk. His day is a mess; he wasn't paying attention, and no, he wasn't trying to kill you.

Pause to absorb knowledge, acceptance, or both. When I struggle with something, it can often take me a while to sort it out. By acknowledging that the problem exists and that it's affecting me, I can move toward accepting it. By accepting a situation, I can reframe my mind and better steel myself to manage my response to its challenges until I can get it figured out and move on.

Talk about your situation with someone who actively listens. This will help you relieve stress because it reinforces—or perhaps reassures—that you are not alone. Resist the urge to fly solo, however difficult it is to be vulnerable. When having a difficult conversation, preface it by saying what you want out of the conversation. You can set the stage for the conversation by stating that you just want to vent and be heard. Likewise, if you want advice, you can let that be known too.

Spend time with loved ones. I struggle with doing this myself, but safe and effective relationships are essential. If your family (or other loved ones) live outside your local area, stay in touch by phone as much as possible. Prioritize spending time with them. Cultivate relationships with people who love and respect you, and have love and respect for them in return.

Take care of yourself. Get plenty of rest, exercise your mind and body, and eat properly. Do things to calm and ground you, such as walking in nature, sitting quietly while focusing on your breath, a favorite hobby, or doing yoga. Our minds need breaks, too. Releasing tension is a great mindfulness exercise to help you drop the nonsense and stress from your brain. Find what works for you, then ease into it. And remind yourself that you deserve it.

Be mindful when dealing with people suffering from stress-related problems. Don't be overly insistent to get them to try things they don't want to do. They are in a world of hurt inside their head. They likely already know what triggers them. Help make the situation less overwhelming. Treat them as you would want to be treated in that same situation. Be a good and supportive listener. Don't try to solve their problems unless they ask you to or give you permission to help.

Do your best to live in the present moment, the here and now. For those who suffer from PTS and other stress-related issues, a normal workload may sometimes seem overwhelming. So, choose one task and work on it. Once you finish a task, such as doing your dishes, pick another, then another. If a certain task causes you anxiety, tell yourself, "It's okay, you've got this." If the anxiety continues, give yourself permission to work on another task. Then, come back to the original task when it feels right. As you do, the progress of checking off tasks may give you a sense of accomplishment and help things feel less overwhelming and more manageable.

Pleasurable activities can help with coping and managing stress. So, make time for them: read a book, go for a walk, catch a movie, spend time in nature, or whatever you find enjoyable. I love watching *America's Got Talent* Golden Buzzer Moments and listening to motivational videos on YouTube. (Pro tip: drug and alcohol dependency are not a part of this since they only mask the pain instead of helping you process it.)

Draw boundaries with yourself. Drawing boundaries can provide essential protection for mental and emotional well-being. We are often told that we need to draw boundaries with other people. That is wrong. We don't draw boundaries with others—we draw boundaries with ourselves. Drawing boundaries with yourself can help you define what you are and are not willing to accept or engage in. It can also help prevent feelings of being overwhelmed by allowing you to prioritize self-care and manage tasks at a comfortable pace. For example, not compromising on your core values can be a boundary.

Don't try to cope alone. Trust me, asking for help is not a sign of weakness. It is a sign of strength—because you just did something that may have been very hard to do. Asking for help when it's hard shows that you can take action to get yourself back on track.

So now that you know what you're preparing for and about the aftermath, let's dive into knowing what to do when life gets hard.

Truth #6: Know What to Do When Life Gets Hard

What do you do when life's difficulties and struggles choose you? What do you do when the tragedy you didn't invite comes knocking on your front door? If you are reading this book, you have likely figured out that life is not easy, and you may be worried about the future. Perhaps you are already in the most difficult seasons of your entire life. How will you respond to guaranteed unwanted struggles and challenges?

When life is difficult, we have the greatest opportunity to make it better.

It requires you to believe in yourself. You need to believe you are capable and ready to give it your all and do your best. The problem you are preparing for might cause worry, fear, anxiety, and incredible stress; your success, however, is not about what's happening externally. It's about what is happening internally.

Just because you *feel* fear doesn't mean you have to *be* afraid. You have the opportunity to recognize the fear, acknowledge it, minimize it, and put it aside. You may feel down and discouraged, but that doesn't have to define who you are. You write your own narrative and define your success, so it's up to you to change it.

It's also up to you to keep showing up when life kicks you in the ass. Remember, you write your own success. Don't give in to the pain, fear, and overwhelm—screw adversity. You can face it. You are prepared. Your life is bigger than this moment or series of events.

You can prove all the doubters wrong—including that part of you that doubted yourself. All you have to do is show up, be the authentic you that you are supposed to be, and keep going. When life gets hard, be successful by believing in yourself, working hard, and trying no matter what.

Life feels good when you accomplish something, especially after struggling to chip away at it until it gets done. If something doesn't make sense, go after it until it does, or at least until it makes better sense. If you decide to give up, question your reason *why*.

There may be some days when the best you can hope for is to make your bed. When life gets hard, dig into your core values. Core values in the form of personal integrity will help you stay true to who you are. Personal honesty will create the opportunity to ask yourself the tough questions and prepare to do the hard things to be ready. Your commitment to personal discipline and integrity will help you establish your new paradigm, your new way of being, and a new norm. Once your new norm is established, you'll have a more progressed and evolved perspective. When your mind guides you through struggles, you will become better at overcoming them regardless of what they are. When life gets hard, take it head-on and dominate it.

Truth #7: Practice Empathy, Grace, and Vulnerability

When preparing for and facing life's hardships, remember to practice empathy, grace, and vulnerability. Kindness and compassion with others—and with yourself—can go a long way toward keeping you true to your core values and, therefore, making your best, most effective decisions. This may seem more ethereal than some other truths presented in this chapter, but it is just as important.

We all live in our version of reality based on and filtered through the impact of the human condition—from within our horizon of lived experience. By practicing empathy, you open yourself up to a greater understanding of the world, partially through another person's perspective. By filtering that through Boyd's Destruction and Creation theory, you can evolve your perspective into something more refined and, ultimately, a better-defined version of reality.

That's why limiting your bias is so important—otherwise, your horizon of lived experience remains narrow, along with your scope of mindset, which hampers your preparedness. Don't let confirmation bias get in the way of being empathetic. If you are true to your core values, you should not fear hearing another perspective. Applying a dose of empathy by actively and honestly listening to and considering someone else's views can feel like a breath of fresh air.

Grace is the acknowledgment of the human condition—giving yourself and others space to screw up without judgment. Instead of viewing something as a failure, you can see it as a lesson learned. Instead of beating yourself up for quitting, acknowledge that it is a temporary stop on the path to a new way of succeeding. Grace does not give you a ticket to be irresponsible. It just means that you acknowledge that you are human and, therefore, will fall short from time to time.

It also means that others will fall short, too. If they have acknowledged it and are attempting to move on in a positive way, we practice grace by giving them the leeway to do so.

When you look for things to be angry and disappointed about (remember confirmation bias), you will surely find them—that's easy to do. The challenge is to find the interesting and positive things in another person and extend grace and forgiveness when it's warranted. Doing that leads to finding the humanity in one another. And it's finding the humanity in others that will help you to find it in yourself. That's not weakness—that just helps you not get stuck carrying the baggage of your anger and disappointment. It helps you understand that we are all fallible, including yourself.

The funny and beautiful thing about grace and empathy is that once you try to put them into practice, you are perfectly positioned to experiment with opening up to other people. You can free yourself from the worry of not measuring up. I'm not saying you should be an emotional sack of tears and rainbows all the time. I'm talking about being more honest in revealing and sharing yourself with the world and those who matter most.

Do you want to be open and live by your core values? Or do you want to hide behind your worry, whether it is legit or not? In my experience, acceptance of my vulnerability makes me more perceptive, and I have become more refined and confident. And confidence is what preparedness is all about.

Truth #8: Take Action

Besides carbon, two other ingredients are needed to make a diamond: pressure and time. These same ingredients also develop amazing people.

Daily life—its struggles, celebrations, and mundane tasks—gives you the opportunity to evolve into a better version of yourself. You can become mentally and physically stronger, add momentum to your life, and propel yourself forward. Perhaps your forward momentum means you are no longer slaving away at a job that you hate (that was mine). Maybe you have finally hit your goal weight and decided to create new fitness goals. Perhaps packing your children's lunches seems boring and routine, but it ensures they have proper food to get them through the day.

Your momentum will carry you out of the ruts of life, but momentum, good or bad, can be tricky. Good momentum requires you to have faith in yourself, and that's not always easy, particularly when you hit a bump in the road. All of us have felt like a loser at some point because our life was momentarily sucking. Hell, I've been in the fetal position because I didn't know how I was going to get the money to feed myself or my animals and keep a roof over our heads.

If you want to change, you have to start somewhere—and you have to be the one to choose to change. No one else can do it for you. You have to find your thing, or a new thing, and go after it. You will have to seek out struggle; it's just a part of it. Anticipate that you will encounter setbacks, and be okay with that. Struggle sets us up for success, and the journey with its highs, lows, and everything in between is the path to success and makes life worth living.

When it comes to preparedness, there comes a time when you stop watching the videos and buying the crap and actually get off your butt and do something about it. The greatest tools you have are your mind and your body, and it's up to you to keep them in top condition. The person in the video does not know your specific situation, and the crap is not useful unless you are using it and understand how it works and why or how it will help you. Being out of shape and unhealthy, when you have a choice and are not doing anything about it, is a choice. And it's a choice not to be as prepared as possible. So lean into your mental and physical preparedness—and do something about it.

Physical exertion is a wanted struggle that gives the mind something else to focus on that isn't your usual day-to-day stress.

Look, I have legendary stare-downs with my front door too; there are days I have to force myself out of it and into the gym, force myself to stretch or walk for twenty minutes, or force myself to do yoga—even though I know that I feel better both physically and mentally when I do these things.

Unfortunately, it's tough for most of us to find the discipline to get up every day and really get after it. Instead, we find excuses. The way around that is through your mindset. It's your mindset that finally kicks in and prompts you to say, *I've had enough, and I'm going to change this.*

Recently, and for the time being, I switched to a mostly Mediterranean diet consisting of fish and fresh vegetables. Now, I'm not a fan of fish, and I can't stand vegetables; however, my struggle to eat healthily is making a difference in my health, fitness, and outlook. When we stop making excuses and start taking action, we feel better. Without being as healthy and fit as possible for your particular situation, you cannot be fully prepared, much less optimally prepared to face the world. Your mindset influences how you're going to approach your challenges, like diet, exercise, and your overall preparedness.

With that, there is a distinction between rest and laziness. Rest is required for your body's restorative processes to do their thing. Laziness is not getting after the things that will keep you healthy, alert, clean, and safe. An occasional morning of sleeping in is not detrimental to your health, but allowing the roof over your head to cave in or leaving your shower floor slippery won't keep you safe.

So, how do you overcome your voice of laziness? How do you truly get prepared? The best way I've found is to set SMART goals:

- ***Specific:*** We often fail to succeed in our goals when we leave them overly broad. In other words, focus on what you must do to achieve your goal. For example, if you want a healthier diet, don't just say, *I want to eat a healthier diet.* Instead, set goals such as *I'm going to eliminate refined sugar from my diet* and *I won't eat after 8 p.m.* Those are specific goals to work toward a healthier lifestyle.
- ***Measurable:*** Sticking with your healthier lifestyle goal, maybe you want to fit into an old pair of jeans or run a marathon. Whatever the case, understanding the *why* behind your goal will help keep you motivated to achieve it.
- ***Attainable:*** Setting unrealistic goals is the recipe for failure. Sure, I would love to climb Mount Everest; however, the chances of me actually doing so at this point in my life are slim to none. Instead, I could commit to hiking a specific number of miles each week or hit a new, more challenging trail each month at a state or local park.
- ***Relevant:*** When you set a goal, you are required to work toward it. Therefore, it has to mean something to you. Relevant motivations are powerful; when the goal matters, you are willing to work at it. Make sure your goals align with your values. Ask yourself, *Is it worth the time*

and effort? Is it worth the effort and personal cost to pursue? Is this goal worth the sacrifice?

- **Time-based:** A goal is not a goal unless you set a timeline for completion. This way, you put yourself on notice that you have work to do, hold yourself accountable, and prioritize your actions. Make sure to select an end date, or it may never be accomplished.

Successful goal-setting is best accomplished with forethought and planning about the areas you need to improve. SMART goal-setting is effective for preparedness-minded people, even the lazy ones. Preparedness-minded people who accomplish their objectives increase their safety, security, and personal resilience; by meeting preparedness goals, they reduce their anxiety and achieve higher confidence levels too.

The Goal of Self, Revisited

What is the goal of self? To be the best *you* possible.

Self is the capability to effectively live your life, to evolve beyond yourself and who you thought you should be, and to go into a new level of being with a greater understanding of the world around you and your relationship within the world. Or, as Maslow put it, self-actualization.

This is intentional and not something you can leave to fate or the universe. If you go back to mindset and how you look at reality, the idea that the planets will suddenly align in your favor isn't reality-based. That may be your perspective, but take it a bit deeper and get personally honest: do you really think the universe will get you to self-actualization? You may live a charmed life where things just seem to work out, but a passive approach to life will not gain you a greater understanding of it.

The fundamentals of preparedness are Mindset, Situational Awareness, Survival, Safety, and Self. You have to prioritize your situational awareness, survival, and safety because if you don't recognize, prepare for, and survive an immediate threat, you may never make it to self. As a result, you don't get to climb Maslow's pyramid, form relationships, have a career, and so on.

Prioritizing is a form of analysis. We only have a finite amount of time on the earth, a finite amount of time each day, and a finite amount of personal energy and resources. Prioritizing allows you to look at what you're doing and determine which courses of action are best for you. You get to choose how to allocate your time, effort, and resources to make the best, most well-informed decisions about what you want to pursue.

Preparedness and Self-Actualization

If you are really prepared, you are saying I am ready to live my best life possible, even if things get bad. It may not be the greatest life compared to what I had, but it's the best life I can live.

When we talk about *survival* and *safety*, we are talking about matters of preparedness: What can I do to prepare? What are my tactics and strategies? When we talk about matters of *self*, we are talking about mindset, and that is one thing you are free to work on anytime, anywhere. All it takes is to keep working through the eight truths outlined in this chapter to connect the dots between self and preparedness.

CONCLUSION

I am often asked, "When it comes to preparing, is there ever a stopping point?" My response is, "Well, do we ever stop learning?" And, for that matter, do we ever stop trying to live a better life?

Learning *is* preparing.

When you go to school, watch a how-to video, or even listen to the Mind4Survival podcast, you are doing something to enhance your life. That is preparedness. Sometimes, it addresses your survival needs, while other times, it addresses your safety and desire to eliminate or minimize unwanted struggle.

So, if you never stop preparing, is there such a thing as being overprepared? Let me put it to you a different way: I don't think you can overprepare; however, I do think you can prepare in a manner that is not congruent with living your best life possible. If you let your quest to prepare for a potential future event that may never happen override the life that you have in the here and now, that's not effective preparedness.

In fact, while you are preparing for a struggle that may not happen, you may inadvertently be causing yourself a mountain of unwanted struggle. For example, many people are so eager to get prepared that they go into debt to do so. They are preparing in fear, thinking they need a bunch of supplies immediately and are willing to max out their credit cards to get it all.

When you hear about the preppers—and I'm speaking as one of them—there are some people who let their fear of what might happen tomorrow destroy their lives today. They move out to the middle of nowhere and live in a place where they struggle, not because they enjoy rural life but because they think they have to be away from people and any outside influences in case something bad happens.

As I've discussed, when you understand that your perspectives are not reality, you can work to arrive at a greater understanding of reality. When you leave a door open for new ideas and perspectives that help you to reevaluate your mindset, you, by default, broaden your horizon of learned experience—and that only serves to develop a stronger mindset and person.

The greatest tools for preparedness are your mindset, understanding, and awareness. They cost nothing but time and mental effort. As long as you keep everything in balance, you can maintain your true self and address your preparedness in a balanced combination of rational thought and emotion. When that happens, your preparations will align with your core values in a way that doesn't cause problems for yourself or others. Instead, you approach life from a mindset of capable confidence rather than anxiety, fear, and worry.

By understanding the goals of preparedness and how they all work together, you realize that they are all pieces of the puzzle.

And as you put them together, you can be thoughtful about what is possible now versus what is possible in the future. Maybe you don't have the money to take in-person training and buy what you want right now. That's okay because there are other things you can do in the meantime to improve your awareness today.

Use the framework laid out in this book to address the things that you can and need to right now and prioritize how to approach the rest.

The Fundamentals of Preparedness

It doesn't matter how rich or poor you are or if you are a Special Operations Forces (SOF) ninja or a single soccer mom trying to figure out how to prepare as the sole breadwinner. The fundamentals always apply, and improving them and your capability doesn't have to cost you a dime.

Whether at your best or in the middle of your worst, the fundamentals of Mindset, Situational Awareness, Survival, Safety, and Self are always applicable. As such, when in doubt or looking to level up your preparedness, always be ready to ask yourself:

- *Am I in the right mindset?*
- *Am I in touch with what's happening around me?*
- *Am I as ready as possible to survive in the moment?*
- *Am I on top of my risk profile?*
- *Am I leading my best life?*

Keep Going!

When we talk about leveling up preparedness, this book is a great starting point, but it's not the finish line. All of the information contained here comes from my perspective, within my horizon of lived experience. Other people have other experiences—and other perspectives. Most have valid reasons for believing and having the perspectives that they do.

Leveling up requires you to analyze the information you take in, look at it critically, and then evaluate it in terms of your experiences and approaches. Remember to stay personally honest and question yourself while you are questioning others. This is how you broaden *and* refine your perspective. See what overlays, what jives, what creates new things, and what creates synergy, and make it your own.

If you constantly go back in and refine your preparedness, you will level up your ability to provide lifesaving skills, resources, and improvements that give you a better life. It's not just beans, bullets, and Band-Aids—improvement *is* preparedness. Anytime you improve, you are improving your preparedness. Keep going, keep reaching—drop me a line at Mind4Survival.com, and let's riff on some preparedness and mindset.

For now, we have arrived at the end of this particular journey, and I'm worn out in a very good way. I'm also grateful that we walked this path together. My hope is that you take this information and make it yours. Now, as for me, I'm going back to being just another prepper trying to live my best life possible, and I will close the same way I sign off on my podcasts:

Stay safe, secure, and prepared. And never forget ... you're just one prep away from being better prepared. *Bye for now.*

HOW TO GET MORE HELP

Throughout this book, I've talked about the importance of preparedness. The goal has always been to equip you with the knowledge and confidence to face life's uncertainties without fear or anxiety. Now, as you stand at the threshold of taking actionable steps, choosing the right resources that fit your journey is crucial. Whether you're just beginning to explore preparedness or looking to deepen your capability, I've designed tools and programs to support you every step of the way. If that's you, I want to offer you a variety of options, from a free checklist to my flagship program or done-for-you preparation consulting services.

Free Basic Emergency Kit Checklist

The best first step is to ensure you've downloaded my free Basic Emergency Kit Checklist, which will walk you through building a basic seven-day emergency kit for you and your family.

Download it here:

www.mind4survival.com/startprepping

"Be Prepared, Not Scared" 6-Week Boot Camp

This is my foundational program for everyone who wants to keep their family safe without wasting time and money. Sign up for our next "Be Prepared, Not Scared" (BPNS) Boot Camp to jump-start your preparedness and be ready for whatever may happen.

Week 1: (Mindset, Situational Awareness, and Risk Management)

Jump-start your preparedness journey with Week 1 of the BPNS Boot Camp. You'll thoroughly understand the fundamentals of preparedness, the importance of mindset, and how to make yours more resilient. We'll also take a deep, easy-to-follow dive into situational awareness and how to improve yours so that you feel more confident and one step ahead. Finally, you'll learn the basics of risk management to have a clear picture of your most significant risks.

Week 2: (Personal Safety and Risk Management)

We'll start Week 2 by focusing on the foundational aspects of preparedness—personal safety and security. Personal safety and security teaches you how to best protect yourself, regardless of your situation. We'll discuss strategies for building individual resilience and ensuring that you are as ready as possible to deal with any challenges that come your way.

Week 3: (Home Preparedness)

Week 3 covers the critical area of home preparedness. We'll review some practical, low-cost tips to make your home a fortress (without looking like a fortress). This week also teaches options for managing your health, hygiene, medical, and shelter needs to keep yourself and your family safe and healthy during an emergency.

Week 4: (Food, Water, and Sleep)

In Week 4, you'll discover strategies to ensure you have the necessary resources to maintain a life that is as normal as possible for you and your loved ones, regardless of the situation around you. You'll also learn what resources you need, how much you need, and how to create a contingency plan so that you and your family have the things you need most—when you need them most.

Week 5: (Family, Finance, and Legal)

You shore up your family, finance, and legal preparedness in Week 5. We discuss how you teach your children to prepare without scaring them. Next, we provide tips to help get your loved ones on board with preparedness. When it comes to finances, we cover topics such as how to make the most out of your preparedness dollar. We'll also discuss the importance of community support and building strong connections.

Week 6: (Community and Course Wrap-Up)

In the final week, we'll tie everything together, focusing on the top level of the survival pyramid: community. We'll then wrap it up with a discussion on how to implement what you've learned and what the next steps are on your preparedness journey.

Bonus #1: Long-Term Disaster Preparedness Module. This module is designed to address the needs of families during prolonged emergencies. Topics include essential considerations for families with small children, how to fortify your home against significant threats, long-term food stockpiling, managing medication supplies over extended periods, and long-term water storage solutions.

Bonus #2: Exclusive access to the BPNS members-only Facebook Community, where I actively lead discussions, provide insights, and moderate conversations. Join a supportive group where you can connect with others, share experiences, and receive direct feedback and advice from me.

Bonus #3: Join our monthly live call, where I will share my valuable insights, answer your pressing questions, and provide personalized advice to help you stay prepared and confident. Don't miss this opportunity to connect directly with an expert dedicated to helping you be prepared, not scared.

Bonus #4: BPNS Boot Camp members get priority access to one-on-one consulting services with me. Enjoy the exclusive benefit of scheduling your personalized sessions ahead of others, ensuring you get the dedicated time and attention needed to enhance your preparedness. This priority access allows you to dive deeper into your specific needs and receive expert guidance tailored just for you.

Join Us Today!

www.mind4survival.com/bootcamp

Personalized Preparedness Coaching and Consulting

Due to high demand, my one-on-one coaching and consulting space is limited, as I can only partner with a small number of clients each year. This is a premium offer for those who wish to streamline their preparedness journey without navigating the complexities alone. Work closely with me to create a tailored preparedness plan, or have it done for you. I provide step-by-step guidance as your coach and consultant. If you are ready for personalized coaching or consulting to enhance your preparedness:

Apply Here!

www.mind4survival.com/consulting

AUTHOR'S NOTE

Here we are, at the end of what has been an incredible—but wanted—struggle for me.

And I have a confession to make. Had I known the scope of struggle that would be involved in getting here, I'm not sure I would have committed to making this book happen. While I knew what I wanted, I didn't realize I had no idea how to make it all work. I wanted and thought I knew how to organize my view on preparedness to help others refine their perspective on how their lives and preparedness intertwine. I knew the fundamental building blocks were there. There was Boyd, Maslow, and Endsley. There was the Survival Rule of Threes and years of failures and successes.

I had the knowledge and the experience. What I didn't have was a way to present it. Nor did I understand how to explain my thoughts in a meaningful way that connects beyond a superficial level. When I started to write this book, I didn't realize that I would have to force myself to sit completely submerged, sometimes nearly drowning, in a viscous pool of memories that I'd rather not have to face—or remember. I didn't realize that to truly achieve my goal, I would not only have to submerge myself in the past but also bring my past, kicking and screaming, into the present.

When I think back to when I started this book, I had a completely different vision for it than where I ended up. In a manner of thinking, I walked through my process repeatedly as I wrote each chapter time and again and moved toward something bigger and more evolved. In my self-actualization journey, I have added to and subtracted from myself in ways I could never have predicted.

Today, I feel a different peace than I felt in the beginning. I have learned to accept that I am just being the best me possible, living the best life possible. Life is relatively enjoyable most days as long as I stick to my core values and try not to disappoint myself.

Funny how that works—when you throw off the bullshit that society tries to heap on you and just be yourself, you eliminate an enormous amount of unwanted struggle! I hope that this book has helped put you on a path to make yourself a better you, too. And maybe, on your very last day, taking your very last breath, you will do so knowing that you are happy and thinking, *You know what? I LIVED A GREAT LIFE!*

Help Spread the Word

I hope you've found this book interesting, entertaining, and helpful. If that's the case, it brings me great joy. I would be even happier if you could help spread the word about

Mind4Survival. You can do this by gifting this book to friends who might benefit from it and leaving an honest five-star rating and kind review where you purchased it. Your support in this way would mean a lot to me. Thank you in advance for helping to share the message!

ACKNOWLEDGMENTS

First, thanks to all of you who have decided to, at minimum, dig deeper and refine your perspective on self-reliance. The fact that you made it this far says something about you. You're not a quitter. You're willing to lean into what many find uncomfortable and put in the time and effort to improve yourself and your situation. That is motivating, and you are why I do what I do.

I want to extend my deepest thanks to my team of friends who have been instrumental in refining this book to its current state. Chris, Daisy, Holly, Dakota, Ed, Josh, and Tristan, your contributions have been invaluable. I couldn't have achieved this without your insightful read-throughs, thought-provoking debates, and fantastic feedback. Each of you has played a crucial role in shaping this book, and I am truly grateful for your support and dedication.

I would be remiss if I didn't thank Alana Jackson, Amy Crawford, and the fantastic team of therapists who helped me through my darkest chapter. The world is brighter and more amazing than I could have imagined. Thank you for saving my life!

In that vein, I also need to thank my four-legged, furry angel, Koah. You came into my life when I needed you most and stayed with me until I was ready to do it on my own. I miss you, buddy!

Dale Goodwin of SurvivalistPrepper.net, thank you for helping me get my start in the online preparedness world.

To my business mentors and friends, Lucy Kelly and Salome Schillack, thank you for your incredible support and guidance. You both truly shine and succeed!

Thanks to my Las Vegas family, Janet and Nick, for everything—you're amazing!

Darrian, thank you for being the best of friends, even when I didn't earn it. You're the best!

Thank you to the Flannery Family for being truly amazing! I love you guys!

Lastly, to both of my moms. Thank you so much for all of your struggle and sacrifice. I wouldn't be the person I am today without you—I love you!

GLOSSARY

360-Degree Preparedness Being as prepared as possible so you're ready regardless of the circumstances.

"Aha!" moment An epiphany or sudden realization. For example, the moment when we realize and accept that we may not be as prepared as we wish we were.

Ability Having the knowledge, skill, and resources to do something

$$\text{Knowledge} \times \text{Skill} \times \text{Resources} = \text{Ability}$$

Asset Someone or something that has emotional or physical value

Capability The ability to do something

$$\text{Mindset} \times \text{Ability} = \text{Capability}$$

Controllable Factors of Success The factors of success that we can control—mindset and ability. Because we can control these factors, the effort we put into them can positively influence our opportunity to succeed.

Cognitive Bias The way a particular person understands events, facts, and other people, which is based on their own particular set of beliefs and experiences, and may not be reasonable or accurate.

Confirmation Bias The cognitive bias that causes people to favor information that confirms their preexisting beliefs, and they seek this information out almost exclusively.

Core Values A person's fundamental beliefs which guide their actions, decisions, and priorities throughout life.

Dialectic Two opposing points that can be both true and present at the same time

Dunning-Krueger Effect A cognitive bias in which people believe they are more capable than they are

Factors of Success Mindset, Ability, and Luck (good or bad)

First Goal of Preparedness Survival

Goals of Preparedness Survival, minimizing unwanted struggle, and living your best possible life

Homeostasis A state of balance among all the body systems needed for the body to survive and function correctly

Hypothermia A medical emergency when a human body's core temperature drops below 95°F (35°C)

Heat Cramps Painful, short-lived cramps often involving the calves, thighs, and shoulders

Heat Exhaustion A medical emergency when a person's core body temperature rises to between 101°F (38°C) and 104°F (40°C)

Impact The consequence of an asset suffering harm

The Human Condition The human condition encompasses the full, unavoidable range of human nature, including personality traits, life experiences, beliefs, fears, etc.

Luck The uncontrollable factor of success. Because it is uncontrollable, it should never be counted on.

Mindset Our mental readiness and awareness shape how we make sense of and interpret ourselves, the world around us, and our situation within that world. Mindset is a controllable factor of success.

Normalcy Bias The bias that makes it difficult for us to engage in "worst-case" thinking and plan for a serious failure or disaster.

Objective Reality True reality. Reality as it exists outside of our perspective-filled thought

OODA Loop A decision-making model known as the OODA Loop which stands for Observe, Orient, Decide, and Act. Created by retired US Air Force Col. John Boyd

Opportunity The likelihood of a beneficial event

Perception The biased lens through which we gain awareness or understanding. The way we think and understand. The act of perceiving.

Perspective A belief or opinion that is influenced by perception

Preparedness All the efforts taken to ensure survival, minimize unwanted struggle, and live your best possible life.

Preparedness Perspective A belief or opinion that does not rely on fact to determine a person's level of preparedness. This leads many people to believe they are prepared when they are actually unprepared.

Resources The external components we use to succeed in the goals of preparedness

$$\text{Quantity} \times \text{Quality} = \text{Resource Capability}$$

Risk The likelihood of a harmful event

Risk Factors Threat, vulnerability, and impact that together determine our risk

Risk Formula The formula, made up of the risk factors, used to determine the risk score of an asset.

$$\text{Threat} \times \text{Vulnerability} \times \text{Impact} = \text{Risk Score}$$

Risk Management The continuous process of evaluating and addressing risk

Risk Profile An objective and continually evolving representation of everything we have to protect, everything we're protecting it from, everything we're protecting it with, and the consequence should we lose what we're protecting.

Risk Register A hierarchical list of assets prioritized by individual risk scores based on the culmination of the three primary factors of risk: threat, vulnerability, and impact.

Risk Score The individual risk score of assets as determined by the risk formula

RPG Rocket Propelled Grenade

Safety Needs The human need for a safe, orderly, predictable, organized world. -Abraham Maslow

Second Goal of Preparedness Minimize unwanted struggle

SHTF (Shit Hit the Fan) An event or situation that overwhelms services and resources, resulting in a collapse of civil order and society.

Situational Awareness The perception of the elements in the environment within a volume of time and space.

Situational Baseline The level norm of our personal environment

SMART Goals A method of achieving our goals. SMART Goals are: Specific, Measurable, Attainable, Relevant, Time-based

Success Formula The formula that, based on capability and luck, determines our chances to be successful at anything

$$\text{Capability} + \text{Luck}^{+/-} = \text{Chance of Success}$$

Survival A two-step process: avoid massive trauma and maintain homeostasis

Third Goal of Preparedness Live your best possible life

Threat A person with ill intent or a hazard such as a natural disaster or another unlucky event

Uncontrollable Factor of Success Luck, both good and bad, is uncontrollable. Therefore, it should never be counted on.

Unwanted Struggle Something you are forced to endure

Vulnerability A lack of preparedness, and whereas preparedness is a measurement of one's capability to mitigate and recover from harm, vulnerability is the inability to prepare for, defend against, and recover from it.

Wanted Struggle Something you choose to endure

ABOUT THE AUTHOR

Brian Duff is a former firefighter-paramedic, Army Ranger, diplomatic protection specialist, and international security director. As a lifelong preparedness advocate, PTS survivor, author, and host and founder of the *Mind4Survival* podcast and website, Brian draws on his lifetime of near misses, close calls, and lucky mistakes to advance his crusade for empowering people to become safer, confident, and self-reliant.

Brian's preparedness experiences range from his early years as a lifeguard and cutting his paramedic teeth in South Central Los Angeles to his service with the 75th Ranger Regiment. He spent over a decade deploying overseas with the U.S. Department of State. Some of Brian's positions include running medical clinics in Afghanistan and Uzbekistan, working as a protective security specialist with Blackwater in Iraq, working with a group of military advisors to the Sudanese People's Liberation Army, operating as a tactical paramedic with the Department of State in Peshawar, Pakistan, and finally managing the security force at the U.S. Embassy in Baghdad.

Following his time overseas, Brian returned to Washington, D.C., where he oversaw a $1B+ government security program and went on to become the director of North American Rescue's education and training center. He is certified as a Project Management Professional and holds a bachelor's degree in security management and a master's in business administration (MBA).

Brian currently lives in Texas, pondering perspectives and surfing this thing we call life. If nothing else, it's all an experience—we might as well try to make it the best experience possible.

www.ingramcontent.com/pod-product-compliance
Lightning Source LLC
Chambersburg PA
CBHW060947050426
42337CB00052B/1625

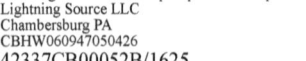